Nuclear Power

Energy and the Environment

ReferencePoint
Press®

San Diego, CA

Select* books in the Compact Research series include:

Current Issues

Abortion
Animal Experimentation
Cloning
Conflict in the Middle East
DNA Evidence and
 Investigation
Drugs and Sports
Energy Alternatives
Gangs
Genetic Testing
Global Warming and
 Climate Change

Immigration
Islam
National Security
Nuclear Weapons and
 Security
Obesity
Online Social Networking
Stem Cells
Teen Smoking
Terrorist Attacks
Video Games
World Energy Crisis

Diseases and Disorders

ADHD
Mood Disorders
Anorexia
Bipolar Disorders
HPV

Obsessive-Compulsive
 Disorder
Post-Traumatic Stress
 Disorder
Self-Injury Disorder
Sexually Transmitted
 Diseases

Drugs

Antidepressants
Club Drugs
Cocaine and Crack
Hallucinogens
Heroin
Inhalants
Marijuana

Methamphetamine
Nicotine and Tobacco
Painkillers
Performance-Enhancing
 Drugs
Prescription Drugs
Steroids

Energy and the Environment

Biofuels
Coal Power
Deforestation
Hydrogen Power

Nuclear Power
Solar Power
Toxic Waste
Wind Power

*For a complete list of titles please visit www.referencepointpress.com.

Nuclear Power

Jill Karson

Energy and the Environment

ReferencePoint
Press®

San Diego, CA

For more information, contact:
ReferencePoint Press, Inc.
PO Box 27779
San Diego, CA 92198
www.ReferencePointPress.com

Picture credits:
Cover: Dreamstime and iStockphoto.com
Maury Aaseng: 32–35, 47–48, 61–63, 75–78
AP Images: 19
Science Photo Library: 17

LIBRARY OF CONGRESS CATALOGING-IN-PUBLICATION DATA

Karson, Jill.
   Nuclear power / by Jill Karson.
      p. cm. — (Compact research series)
   Includes bibliographical references and index.
   ISBN-13: 978-1-60152-123-1 (hardback : alk. paper)
   ISBN-10: 1-60152-123-5 (hardback : alk. paper)
   1. Nuclear energy—Juvenile literature. I. Title.
   TK9148.C37   2011
   333.792'4—dc22
                                                2010010108

Contents

Foreword

A s modern civilization continues to evolve, its ability to create, store, distribute, and access information expands exponentially. The explosion of information from all media continues to increase at a phenomenal rate. By 2020 some experts predict the worldwide information base will double every 73 days. While access to diverse sources of information and perspectives is paramount to any democratic society, information alone cannot help people gain knowledge and understanding. Information must be organized and presented clearly and succinctly in order to be understood. The challenge in the digital age becomes not the creation of information, but how best to sort, organize, enhance, and present information.

ReferencePoint Press developed the *Compact Research* series with this challenge of the information age in mind. More than any other subject area today, researching current issues can yield vast, diverse, and unqualified information that can be intimidating and overwhelming for even the most advanced and motivated researcher. The *Compact Research* series offers a compact, relevant, intelligent, and conveniently organized collection of information covering a variety of current topics ranging from illegal immigration and deforestation to diseases such as anorexia and meningitis.

The series focuses on three types of information: objective single-author narratives, opinion-based primary source quotations, and facts and statistics. The clearly written objective narratives provide context and reliable background information. Primary source quotes are carefully selected and cited, exposing the reader to differing points of view. And facts and statistics sections aid the reader in evaluating perspectives. Presenting these key types of information creates a richer, more balanced learning experience.

For better understanding and convenience, the series enhances information by organizing it into narrower topics and adding design features that make it easy for a reader to identify desired content. For example, in *Compact Research: Illegal Immigration*, a chapter covering the economic impact of illegal immigration has an objective narrative explaining the various ways the economy is impacted, a balanced section of numerous primary source quotes on the topic, followed by facts and full-color illustrations to encourage evaluation of contrasting perspectives.

The ancient Roman philosopher Lucius Annaeus Seneca wrote, "It is quality rather than quantity that matters." More than just a collection of content, the *Compact Research* series is simply committed to creating, finding, organizing, and presenting the most relevant and appropriate amount of information on a current topic in a user-friendly style that invites, intrigues, and fosters understanding.

Nuclear Power at a Glance

The Power of Fission

Nuclear power comes from the energy stored deep in the nucleus of an atom. Splitting the nucleus, a process called fission, creates a burst of energy in the form of heat. This is the source of nuclear power.

Harnessing Nuclear Power

The nuclear fuel uranium undergoes fission in a nuclear reactor at a power plant that is similar to a traditional power plant. The only difference is that the steam that drives the turbines that generate electricity is created from the heat produced by fission.

Energy Production

According to the Nuclear Energy Institute, the U.S. fleet of 104 nuclear reactors generates about 20 percent of the nation's electricity. Worldwide, 436 nuclear reactors generate about 15 percent of the world's electricity supply each year.

Nuclear Oversight

A framework of national and international laws and agreements governs all phases of nuclear power generation and usage. Governing bodies include the U.S. Nuclear Regulatory Commission and the International Atomic Energy Agency.

Environmental Impact

Unlike fossil fuel–based plants, nuclear power plants do not produce carbon dioxide or other greenhouse gases during routine operation.

Radioactive Waste

The nuclear process produces long-lived radioactive waste that must be sequestered for many years. In the United States this waste is currently stored at 131 sites in 39 states. The waste will remain in these interim facilities while the nuclear industry develops plans for a long-term geological repository.

Other Uses

Aside from electricity generation, nuclear technology has numerous applications in medicine, research, and industry.

Nuclear Proliferation

The uranium and plutonium used in a nuclear reactor could also be used to fabricate nuclear weapons; these materials must be heavily guarded so that they are not diverted for weapons use.

Overview

Nearly one-fifth of the world's electricity is generated at the 436 nuclear power plants operating worldwide today. Nuclear power comes from the tremendous energy that is stored in the center part, or nucleus, of an atom. Infinitesimally tiny atoms make up everything in the universe. Still smaller particles, protons and neutrons, form the atom's core, or nucleus. These particles are bound tightly together, keeping the nucleus intact; in fact, the nucleic bonds of most elements are simply too powerful to break. Certain elements such as uranium, however, have large, unstable nuclei that can be split apart—a process known as nuclear fission. The immense energy set free when an atom fissions is the source of nuclear power.

The Birth of the Atomic Age

Although people have known about atoms for thousands of years, the discovery of atomic fission—and the ability to harness the abundant energy it produces—is a relatively recent phenomenon. In 1938 the German scientists Otto Hahn and Fritz Strassmann first discovered that the nucleus of a uranium atom splits when it is hit by a neutron. While these and other early experiments contributed significantly to an understanding of nuclear processes, the advent of World War II—and the knowledge that Nazi Germany was conducting nuclear experiments—provided the impetus to accelerate nuclear research in the United States. As the renowned scientist Albert Einstein wrote to U.S. president Franklin Roosevelt: "It may be possible to set up a nuclear reaction in uranium . . . [that] would also lead to the construction of . . . extremely powerful bombs of a new type."[1] With the specter of a nuclear-armed Germany looming, Roosevelt launched the Advisory Committee on Uranium in October 1939. It was later renamed the Manhattan Project. The race to create a bomb using the power from an atom's nucleus was underway.

Pivotal to the success of the Manhattan Project were the discoveries of the Italian scientist Enrico Fermi, who created the first controlled nuclear chain reaction using uranium atoms. In a chain reaction, the neutrons released from one split uranium atom go on to hit and split other atoms. These neutrons start more fissions, which produce more neutrons, and so on. The amount of nuclear fuel required to create and sustain a chain reaction is called the critical mass—that is, a mass sufficiently large to ensure that neutrons from one uranium atom would hit another uranium atom and keep the process going.

> **Nearly one-fifth of the world's electricity is generated at the 436 nuclear power plants operating worldwide today.**

Working at the University of Chicago in 1942, Fermi demonstrated the process. To regulate the fission reaction, Fermi placed control rods made of cadmium in a pile of fissile material (that is, material that undergoes fission). Because cadmium is able to absorb neutrons, it can be used to start and stop the fission process. When Fermi pulled the control rods out of his pile, the fission chain reaction built rapidly, producing enormous amounts of energy. When he reinserted the rods, the cadmium started absorbing neutrons, bringing the fission process to a halt. Fermi speculated that in a nuclear bomb, the chain reaction could be allowed to go unchecked; without control rods to stop the process, the mass of uranium would get so hot that it would eventually explode. A weapon that employed such an uncontrolled nuclear reaction would be 20 million times stronger than the most powerful explosives used at the time. Under the direction of J. Robert Oppenheimer, who headed the Manhattan Project, Fermi and a host of American and European scientists built on these discoveries to secretly design and test the bombs that would ultimately end World War II.

> " The mushroom clouds that exploded over Japan provided a vivid—and uniquely terrifying—example of unrestrained nuclear power. "

By the time the bombs were complete, the United States and its allies had won the war in Europe; Japan, however, refused to surrender. On August 6, 1945, the crew of the plane *Enola Gay* dropped the world's first atomic bomb on Hiroshima, Japan, instantly killing over 70,000 people. Two days later, a second bomb killed another 30,000 people when it was dropped on the Japanese city of Nagasaki. The war was over, and the atomic age was born.

From Military Weapon to Electricity

With the advent of the atomic age came intense fears about nuclear power and its life-destroying capabilities. The mushroom clouds that exploded over Japan provided a vivid—and uniquely terrifying—example of unrestrained nuclear power. At the same time, Fermi's discovery that the nuclear process could be started and stopped at will demonstrated its potential application as a powerful energy source for peacetime civilian use. To this end, the U.S. Congress passed the Atomic Energy Act in 1946, thereby establishing the Atomic Energy Commission to oversee the development and use of nuclear technology. On December 8, 1953, President Dwight Eisenhower gave his famous Atoms for Peace address to the United Nations. Exhorting the nations of the world that were pursuing nuclear technology to "strip its military casing and adapt it to the arts of peace," Eisenhower stated: "The United States knows that if the fearful trend of atomic military build-up can be reversed, this greatest of destructive forces can be developed into a great boon, for the benefit of all mankind. The United States knows that peaceful power from atomic energy is not a dream of the future. The capability, already proved, is here today."[2]

The president's Atoms for Peace program ushered in an era during which nuclear power would be developed for peaceful purposes—namely electricity generation. At the same time, it kept America at the fore of nuclear development. In 1954 Congress amended the Atomic Energy Act, granting the Atomic Energy Commission the power to license private companies to build and operate commercial nuclear power plants. The boom in nuclear power plant development that followed led to an increasing demand for uranium, the primary fuel used in nuclear power plants today.

The Nuclear Fuel Process

Uranium is the most practical and most commonly used nuclear fuel for several reasons. Uranium is the heaviest element found in nature. The energy required to hold uranium's abundant atomic particles together is huge; this powerful "binding energy" is what is released during the fission process. At the same time, uranium is naturally radioactive—that is, atoms of uranium are unstable and can be broken apart. It is so fissile that a self-sustaining nuclear chain reaction—in which neutrons split, fire off, and go on to split other nuclei to keep the process going—can be easily maintained in a nuclear reactor. Once initiated, the nuclear chain reaction is extraordinarily efficient. One pound (0.45kg) of uranium that has undergone fission produces as much energy as that produced by 150,000 tons (136,078 metric tons) of coal.

In its pure form, uranium is a shiny silver metal that occurs in soil, rock, and water. Pitchblende is the primary uranium ore—the rocks that contain uranium. The pure uranium in the ore is so sparse that a pile of pitchblende the size of a small building must be dug out of the earth to produce a fist-size lump of uranium. At the same time, uranium, like many elements, exists in several isotopes, each

> **Once initiated, the nuclear chain reaction is extraordinarily efficient.**

of which has a slightly different number of neutrons in its nuclei. The isotope that will most easily undergo fission is uranium-235, which must be separated from the more abundant uranium-238, which makes up approximately 99 percent of the world's supply of the element. Uranium deposits are present across the globe, with large reserves in Canada, Kazakhstan, and Australia producing a large quantity of the world's supply. Once mined, the uranium ore is separated, purified, and processed into small pellets that can be used to create a nuclear chain reaction deep inside the steel cylinders of a nuclear reactor.

The Nuclear Power Plant

Traditional power plants burn fuel such as coal to boil water into superheated steam. The steam blasts at high pressure against the blades of a turbine, which in turn spins the shaft of a generator to produce electricity. A nuclear power plant is no different, except that the steam is created with the heat that is produced by the controlled nuclear fission chain reaction of radioactive fuel, usually uranium-235. This chain reaction takes place within a reactor core and is regulated by moderators, typically graphite rods or water, which slow fast-moving neutrons to a speed suitable for fission to occur. Just as Fermi demonstrated in 1942, control rods, composed of materials such as cadmium or boron, absorb spare neutrons and thereby adjust the rate of fission—and hence the amount of heat produced. If a reaction is going too far, for example, control rods are lowered into the reactor core to capture the excess neutrons and decelerate the process. As heat is created, it is transferred to water to produce the steam that will power the turbines linked to the electricity generator.

> Nuclear reactors differ in their shape and design, although they operate under the same underlying principle—the controlled splitting of the nuclei of radioactive atoms to produce heat.

Nuclear reactors differ in their shape and design, although they operate under the same underlying principle—the controlled splitting of the nuclei of radioactive atoms to produce heat. There are two types of nuclear reactors: fast reactors and thermal reactors. Fast reactors use a mixture of uranium and plutonium as fuel. Since plutonium fissions easily, moderators are not needed to slow down neutrons—hence, "fast neutrons" produce the fissions that generate heat. Fast reactors, also called breeder reactors, use some of the energy released to produce, or "breed," more fuel than they use.

> " In the United States 104 nuclear power plants generate nearly 20 percent of the nation's energy. "

Most nuclear power plants use thermal reactors, in which chain reactions are produced by slow-moving, or thermal, neutrons. Many different types of thermal reactors are in service throughout the world. The differences in the various designs are found primarily in the coolants and composition of the fuels they use. There are two main types of thermal reactors: the pressurized water reactor and the boiling water reactor. The pressurized water reactor is the world's most widely used reactor type. Whereas a boiling water reactor generates steam directly in the reactor, the pressurized water reactor keeps the radioactive water in the reactor core under extreme pressure so that it does not boil. Rather, it goes through a heat exchanger that transfers its heat to clean water, which in turn creates the steam that generates the electricity.

Is Nuclear Power a Viable Energy Source?

Today nuclear power plants produce over 15 percent of the world's electricity. In the United States 104 nuclear power plants generate nearly 20 percent of the nation's energy. It is fossil fuels, however, that generate the largest share of electricity in most countries. Worldwide, fossil fuels supply close to 70 percent of the energy consumed. Fossil fuels—primarily coal, oil, and gas—are so called because they have been formed from the fossilized remains of plants and animals that lived during the Carboniferous period 360 to 286 million years ago, although the age of some organisms exceeds 600 million years. Because the geological forces that create fossil fuels require hundreds of millions of years, these fuels cannot be replaced when the supply runs out.

> **Because nuclear reactors do not release CO_2 during routine operations, many believe that nuclear power has a crucial role in a low-carbon-energy future.**

Although fossil fuels are indeed the dominant source of energy today, the reserves of fossil fuels are finite, and once depleted they are gone forever. For example, according to some estimates, oil reserves will be seriously depleted within 45 years and gas in 65 years. Also, the United States imports much of its oil from politically unstable parts of the world such as the Middle East, where close to 70 percent of the world reserve of oil is concentrated. Another disadvantage to using fossil fuels to generate electricity is that when they are burned, they release large amounts of carbon dioxide (CO_2) and other pollutants into the atmosphere.

Senator Pete Domenici of New Mexico, author of the book *A Brighter Tomorrow: Fulfilling the Promise of Nuclear Energy*, states:

> The grim picture is that today's sources of fossil fuels are universally agreed to be pollutants and contributors of greenhouse gas emissions and acid rain, particularly coal and oil. . . . Especially worrisome are the geopolitical, resource adequacy, and environmental issues surrounding the continued use of fossil fuels. . . . We in the United States also know that our country is overly dependent upon foreign countries for increasing supplies of oil. . . . These resource, security, and environmental concerns lead me to conclude that nuclear power could be a heaven-sent alternative to polluting fossil fuels for energy supply in this century.[3]

Like Domenici, many scientists, government officials, and private citizens believe that nuclear power is an attractive option in a world in which current energy supplies are uncertain and the environmental consequences of fossil fuel combustion are potentially dire. Others vehemently disagree, and indeed, nuclear power has received more public attention and debate—usually polarizing and highly emotional—than any other energy source to date. Public perception on a variety of issues, including reactor safety, waste disposal, nuclear economics, and energy security, will largely determine whether nuclear power will play a meaningful role in a transition away from fossil fuels in the coming decades.

How Does Nuclear Power Affect the Environment?

The most pressing environmental concern of the day is global warming, the increase in the average temperature of the earth's atmosphere and oceans that many believe to be a direct result of greenhouse gas emissions, primarily CO_2, into the atmosphere. While the causes and effects

A storage facility in France holds barrels of low-level nuclear waste created by the incineration of components used in the nuclear fuel cycle. The nuclear fuel process produces long-lived radioactive waste that must be sequestered for many years.

of the earth's changing climate are uncertain, most agree that increasing temperatures are causing serious repercussions, such as rising sea levels and changes in the intensity and duration of hurricanes and other weather events. Measures to combat global warming often focus on finding less-polluting options to traditional fossil fuel–based power plants, which produce hundreds of thousands of tons of CO_2 each year. Because nuclear reactors do not release CO_2 during routine operations, many believe that nuclear power has a crucial role in a low-carbon-energy future.

On the other hand, if nuclear power is to gain widespread support as a practical way to tackle global warming, the issue of nuclear waste must be effectively addressed. Because the spent fuel rods and other by-products of the nuclear fuel process are highly radioactive, these materials must be safely contained for tens of thousands of years, periods "longer than the history of most governments the world has seen,"[4] as one former Atomic Energy Commission chief put it. Many worry that any number of unforeseen events—natural disasters like earthquakes or floods, fires, wars, terrorism, and changes in government, for example—could compromise the stored waste, causing an inadvertent release into the environment, with potentially dire consequences to human health.

Is Nuclear Power Safe?

Nuclear safety concerns often center on the possibility of an uncontrolled release of radiation from a compromised reactor core. Two highly publicized accidents highlighted this potentiality. On March 28, 1979, an accident at the Three Mile Island nuclear plant in Pennsylvania resulted in a partially melted reactor core. Although no one was injured and only small amounts of radiation were released, the accident led many to question the safety of nuclear technology. The world's worst nuclear accident occurred on April 26, 1986, at the Chernobyl facility in Ukraine, where one of the plant's four reactors overheated. The resulting explosion blasted tons of radioactive dust and gas across Europe, providing a prescient demonstration that nuclear safety concerns are global in nature.

In the years since these two incidents, extraordinary efforts have been put forth to enhance operational safety and minimize the probability of reactor core damage. Indeed, the nuclear industry has established a solid safety record over the past two decades. As James Lovelock, an Honorary Visiting Fellow at Oxford University and a longtime environmental

The 1979 accident at Pennsylvania's Three Mile Island nuclear power plant (pictured) proved disastrous to the nascent U.S. nuclear power industry. Although the facility's containment structure performed as designed and no one was injured, the industry could not overcome public safety concerns.

activist, states: "A Swiss study of deaths related to power generation came up with astonishing results. Nuclear turns out to be five times safer than oil, ten times safer than gas and 100 times safer than hydro-electric dams. According to the World Health Organization, worldwide fossil-fuel pollution is responsible for three million deaths a year."[5]

At the same time, many remain skeptical about the nuclear industry's ability to mitigate risks and ensure public safety. As Jim Riccio of Greenpeace states: "The public should not be lulled into a false sense of security by the mere fact that the U.S. nuclear power industry has not melted down a reactor since Three-Mile-Island. Operating without a meltdown for a finite period of time does not mean that safety is adequate."[6]

Today nuclear power plants are strictly regulated, although the regulating body differs by country. The U.S. Nuclear Regulatory Commission oversees all U.S. nuclear power plants, each of which must be licensed, submit to regular inspections, and abide by all legally mandated safety regulations. Smaller regulating agencies operate in some of the 31 U.S. states that have nuclear power plants.

Apart from reactor safety, myriad security issues must be addressed. Specifically, the radioactive materials used to generate electricity can also be used to produce nuclear bombs. Keeping these materials out of the hands of terrorists and rogue states presents formidable challenges. To this end, the International Atomic Energy Agency was established by the United Nations in 1957 to help nations develop nuclear power exclusively for peaceful purposes—and to ensure that nuclear states abide by this commitment.

What Is the Future of Nuclear Power?

In December 2009 close to 100 world leaders gathered in New York for the United Nations Summit on Climate Change, the largest environmental meeting in history. There attendees outlined a plan whereby nations would commit to reducing the greenhouse gas emissions that contribute to global warming. As part of this global initiative, U.S. president Barack Obama submitted a paper to the United Nations outlining his administration's climate goals: that the United States would cut carbon emissions up to 17 percent by 2020, from 2005 levels. The president has stated that he favors the deployment of nuclear power as part of a green energy strategy and to meet the nation's energy needs. At the same time, Obama has resolved not to support growth in the nuclear sector until nuclear waste management and proliferation issues are resolved.

Today the 436 nuclear reactors operating around the globe generate approximately 370 gigawatts of electricity, and as of January 2010 over 50 new reactors were under construction in 16 countries. In the United States, however, there has not been an order for new nuclear plant construction in over three decades. Any large-scale nuclear expansion in the United States will require that formidable issues be addressed. Perhaps most importantly, public confidence in nuclear power—and whether or not the nuclear industry can adopt novel solutions to long-standing problems—will largely determine the extent and scope of nuclear power's role in meeting the country's—and world's—future energy needs.

Is Nuclear Power a Viable Energy Source?

> 66Nuclear power offers a clean and cost-effective answer to many of our nation's current and future energy needs.99
>
> —J. Barnie Beasley Jr., former president of the Southern Nuclear Operating Company.

> 66It is obvious that nuclear power is neither cheap, green, nor sustainable.99
>
> —Helen Caldicott, physician, author, and antinuclear activist.

In August 1951—only six years after the spectacularly destructive capabilities of nuclear power were demonstrated at the close of World War II—the U.S. Navy issued a contract for a new submarine. It was powered by an onboard nuclear reactor, "the basis of the country's infant atomic industry,"[7] as one of the members of Congress present at the vessel's inaugural ceremony commented. Indeed, the commercialization of nuclear power as an energy source was well underway by the early 1950s.

The Rise and Fall of Nuclear Power in America

When construction commenced on the country's first nuclear power plant in Shippingport, Pennsylvania, in 1954, Atomic Energy Commission chair Lewis Strauss offered a prophetic vision of the new enterprise: "It is not too much to expect that our children will enjoy in their homes electrical energy too cheap to meter."[8] The nuclear industry did in fact appear ready to take off. The Shippingport plant was producing electricity by 1957, and between 1965 and 1970, utility companies placed close to 100 orders for reactor construction.

An accident at the Three Mile Island nuclear plant in Pennsylvania in 1979 brought the stellar ascent of the nuclear industry to a screeching halt. Although the facility's containment structure performed as designed and was not breached, and only small amounts of radiation were released into the environment, the incident forever changed the way the public viewed nuclear power. Galvanized opposition coupled with regulatory problems, construction delays, economic hurdles, and other issues that plagued the newly emerging industry proved disastrous. The industry has not yet recovered from the profound change in public opinion that followed Three Mile Island and the far worse accident that occurred seven years later at Chernobyl. No new reactors ordered since the 1970s have been built to completion in the United States, and many states have shut down or halted production of nuclear power.

> **An accident at the Three Mile Island nuclear plant in Pennsylvania in 1979 brought the stellar ascent of the nuclear industry to a screeching halt.**

Senator Pete Domenici describes this impasse as purely political in his book, *A Brighter Tomorrow*: "Three Mile Island, Chernobyl, uninformed hysteria about nuclear power's true risks, and irresponsible decisions by policymakers have made nuclear energy into a pariah in some minds. Pseudoscience has been pumped into our culture like bilge water, flushing out the good science. Thus it has been for three decades in the United States."[9]

Whatever the reality, the nuclear debate remains highly charged and emotional, and the nuclear industry will most certainly need to address public fears about safety if it is to move forward and remain viable.

The World's Growing Energy Demands

According to the U.S. Census Bureau, the world's population will likely increase from roughly 6 billion today to 9 billion by 2050. Although energy forecasts for this growing populace are not strictly quantifiable, the world's energy needs will undoubtedly increase—perhaps dramatically—in coming years. For example, the World Energy Council and other organizations estimate that the consumption of energy will likely double in the next 50 years. Some estimates put this figure even higher. The International Energy Agency projects that most of the growth in demand will come from China, India, and other developing Asian countries, where rapidly growing economies will likely produce heightened standards of living—along with the electricity requirements necessary to maintain these higher standards. As a 2009 report by the International Energy Agency put it: "The global surge in the use of consumer electronics such as flat screen TVs, iPods, and mobile phones will triple electricity consumption by 2030."[10]

> **According to the Independent Electric Power Research Institute, the United States will need to build an additional 45 nuclear plants by the year 2030 to meet its base load energy requirements.**

The magnitude of these enormous energy requirements is inescapable. Currently, fossil fuels generate most of the electricity for the global economy. According to the International Energy Agency, 41.6 percent of the world's electricity was generated by coal in 2007, 20.9 percent by natural gas, and 5.7 percent by oil. Nuclear power, by comparison, generated just under 15 percent of the electricity consumed worldwide the same year.

The Nuclear Industry Today

Nuclear proponents believe that a widely expanded nuclear program will help meet global energy demands as it lessens the world's dependence on fossil fuels. Today nuclear power plants operate in 30 countries, including the United States, where nuclear power is the leading source of electricity after coal, France, Japan, Germany, the United Kingdom, and Russia.

According to the independent Electric Power Research Institute, the United States will need to build an additional 45 nuclear plants by the year 2030 to meet its base load energy requirements—that is, the steady, reliable, around-the-clock power that utilities require to meet customer demands. Since the late 1970s, however, all new plant construction—and the private investment necessary to build new units—has been canceled or delayed indefinitely in the wake of the accident at the Three Mile Island nuclear facility in Pennsylvania. No new nuclear plants have been built to completion since then.

There are some indications that this may be changing. Only one previously ordered nuclear power plant is currently under construction in the United States. However, the U.S. Nuclear Regulatory Commission, the agency that governs domestic nuclear activity, has received applications for construction and licensing of 26 new reactors, although financing and other issues must be resolved before construction commences. Too, the agency extended the operating licenses of 19 plants between January 2003 and February 2008. Lastly, improved operating performance at existing plants has resulted in increased electricity output, making investment in nuclear power more favorable. In the past decade, for example, nuclear power plants have added more than 23,000 megawatts to the domestic electricity supply without new plant construction. This is equivalent to the energy produced at 23 nuclear power plants.

> **Nuclear power can generate electricity 24 hours a day, 7 days a week. It requires little fuel to operate and is extremely efficient.**

By comparison, there are over 50 nuclear plants under construction in 16 countries around the world, including 16 in China, 9 in Russia, and 6 in India. Finland and the United Kingdom, too, have announced plans to add new nuclear facilities. The nuclear industry in France, in particular, is thriving. With almost no natural supplies of fossil fuels, France launched a nuclear program in 1974. Since then it has constructed 59 power plants that today produce over 75 percent of the domestic electricity supply. This makes France the most nuclear-powered country in the world in terms of per capita energy consumption. France even exports large amounts of nuclear-generated electricity to other countries, including Switzerland, Italy, and the United Kingdom. Japan, too, operates a robust nuclear program, with 54 nuclear plants that provide 25 percent of the country's electricity—and construction of new units is underway.

Will Renewable Energy Sources Mitigate the Need for Nuclear Power?

It is universally agreed that renewable energy sources such as solar, wind, geothermal, and hydroelectric power must continue to be developed as part of a sustainable energy future for the United States and the world. Many hope that these renewable sources may negate the need for an expanded nuclear program in coming years. Like nuclear power, however, these alternative sources have their own unique issues—primarily high costs and inefficiency—that must be addressed if they are to be truly viable sources of energy. Sunlight, for example, is too diffuse and intermittent—interrupted by night and cloud cover—for solar power to play a major role in electricity generation. Similarly, wind power cannot provide a continuous, reliable supply of energy because it too is subject to the vagaries of wind patterns. Costs for these technologies are prohibitive as well. By some estimates, for example, solar panels do not even generate enough power over their lifetime to recover even 30 percent of their installation costs.

By comparison, nuclear power can generate electricity 24 hours a day, 7 days a week. It requires little fuel to operate and is extremely efficient. According to the International Atomic Energy Agency, all forms of renewable energy combined accounted for just 1.09 percent of North America's total electricity generation in 2008, compared with 19.04 percent for nuclear energy.

As Peter W. Huber and Mark P. Mills write in their book *The Bottomless Well: The Twilight of Fuel, the Virtue of Waste, and Why We Will Never Run Out of Energy*: "Coal, uranium, and gas plants generate gargantuan amounts of power in very small

> **Carbon taxes or carbon emissions trading—economic incentives to reduce the emissions of CO_2 and other pollutants—may favor nuclear power because it does not produce CO_2 during electricity generation.**

amounts of space. . . . Sun and wind come nowhere close. Earnest though they are, the people who maintain otherwise are the people who brought us 400 million more tons of coal a year."[11]

Advocates of renewable energy sources contend that although they may make up a small share of the energy market today, these energy sources will become more efficient, safer, and economically competitive as technology advances in the coming years. Arjun Makhijani, president of the Institute for Energy and Environmental Research, is among those who believe that alternate energy sources will negate the need for an expansion of nuclear power. Makhijani explains:

> The U.S. renewable energy resource base is vast and untapped. Available wind energy resources in 12 Midwestern and Rocky Mountain states equal about 2.5 times the entire electricity production of the United States. . . . Solar energy resources on just one percent of the area of the United States are about three times as large as wind energy, if production is focused in the high isolation areas in the Southwest and West. . . . With the right combination of technologies, it is likely that even the use of coal can be phased out, along with nuclear electricity.[12]

How Expensive Is Nuclear Power?

Like many issues related to nuclear power, nuclear economics are controversial, largely because quantifying the cost of nuclear-generated power is extremely difficult. Generally, costs are divided into expenses associated with plant construction, plant operation and maintenance, fuel costs, waste disposal, and plant decommissioning. Constructing a nuclear power plant is expensive—indeed, it is the primary cost associated with this energy source. According to former vice president Al Gore:

> The driving force that has converted once vibrant nuclear dreams into debilitating nightmares for electric utilities has been the grossly unacceptable economics of the present generation of reactors. To begin with, the cost of constructing nuclear power plants has escalated wildly, to the point where most utilities have long since abandoned any idea of ordering new reactors.[13]

Capital costs for new plant construction can run as high as $4 billion. Some estimates put the figure as high as $14 billion—costs for which the nuclear industry has received vast government subsidies over the past 50 years. Many believe, however, that these costs will shrink significantly with the growth of the industry, as past experience and increased standardization are applied to the construction of next-generation power plants.

Once a plant is up and running, operating, maintenance, and fuel costs are relatively low by comparison. Nuclear power plants do require unique safeguards, however. Unlike fossil fuel–burning plants, nuclear facilities must be protected from sabotage, including the theft of radioactive material. Too, the radioactive waste produced must be stored—and shielded so that it does not emit radiation—for thousands of years. The cost of transporting, protecting, and storing this waste—although undetermined— must be considered as part of the overall cost. Lastly, plants must be shut down and decommissioned at the end of their life cycle, usually 40 to 60 years. The decommissioning—which may include dismantling, storing, or entombing the reactor—may cost $300 million or more.

Measures to combat global warming may mitigate some of the expenses associated with nuclear power. For example, carbon taxes or carbon emissions trading—economic incentives to reduce the emissions of CO_2 and other pollutants—may favor nuclear power because it does not produce CO_2 during electricity generation. According to a 2008 study by the Congressional Budget Office: "The longer-term competitiveness of nuclear technology as a source of electricity is likely to depend on policymakers' decisions regarding carbon dioxide constraints. If such constraints are implemented, nuclear power will probably enjoy a cost advantage over conventional fossil-fuel alternatives as a source of electricity-generating capacity."[14]

Ascertaining whether nuclear power is a practical way to meet growing energy needs will require continued research, innovation, and a fair assessment of all available evidence in the years to come.

Is Nuclear Power a Viable Energy Source?

> **Realistically, we as a nation have no silver bullets that in the near- or mid-term can replace nuclear power as a reliable, 24/7 producer of massive amounts of . . . electric power.**

—John Grossenbacher, statement made at the U.S. House Committee on Science and Technology hearing, "Opportunities and Challenges for Nuclear Power," April 23, 2008. www.science.house.gov.

Grossenbacher is the director of the Idaho National Laboratory.

> **Replacing coal with nuclear is risky, costly and unnecessary. . . . Renewable energy sources are quite sufficient to provide ample, reliable electricity.**

—Arjun Makhijani, "Nuclear Is Not the Right Energy Source," *Dallas Morning News*, February 26, 2008. www.dallasnews.com.

Makhijani is the president of the Institute for Energy and Environmental Research and the author of *Carbon-Free and Nuclear-Free: A Roadmap for U.S. Energy Policy*.

66 **Nuclear power is the most expensive way ever devised to generate electricity. The method is not anywhere near cost-effective.** 99

—Sierra Club, "Bush Administration's Nuclear Power Plan Ignores True Costs, Missed Opportunities," January 26, 2006. www.sierraclub.org.

The Sierra Club is the largest grassroots environmental organization in the United States. The group opposes building and using nuclear power plants.

66 **Increasing fossil fuel prices have greatly improved the economics of nuclear power for electricity now. Several studies show that nuclear energy is the most cost-effective of the available base-load technologies.** 99

—World Nuclear Association, "World Energy Needs and Nuclear Power," November 25, 2008. www.world-nuclear.org.

The World Nuclear Association is an association of companies that supports the global nuclear energy industry.

66 **Each new nuclear plant takes ten years or more to construct, and a large-scale transition to nuclear power would take decades—time we don't have to spare. Other solutions . . . can be adopted much more quickly.** 99

—Erich Picha, "Nuclear Power: A False Solution to Climate Crisis," *Friends of the Earth*, February 26, 2009. www.foe.org.

Picha is the president of Friends of the Earth, an environmental advocacy group with a network of grassroots groups in 77 countries.

66 **The important and overriding consideration is time: we have nuclear now, and new nuclear building should be started immediately. All of the alternatives . . . require decades of development.** 99

—James Lovelock, *The Revenge of Gaia: Earth's Climate Crisis and the Fate of Humanity*. New York: Basic, 2007.

Lovelock is a British scientist, author, and environmentalist. He has taught at Yale University and Harvard University in the United States.

66 We have a choice to make: We can either continue the 30-year emotional debate about whether we should embrace nuclear energy, or we can accept its practical advantages. **99**

—Christine Todd Whitman, "The Case for Nuclear Power," *Business Week*, September 17, 2007.

Whitman is the former governor of New Jersey and the former U.S. Environmental Protection Agency administrator. She is the current cochair of the Clean and Safe Energy Coalition.

66 History offers plenty of reasons to steer clear of nuclear power and opt instead for the abundant quicker, cheaper, and safer opportunities. **99**

—Walt Patterson, "Nuclear Amnesia," *World Today*, April 2006. www.theworldtoday.org.

Patterson is a fellow of the Energy, Environment and Development Programme at Chatham House, an organization located in the United Kingdom that conducts research and disseminates information on a wide range of issues, including energy and public policy.

66 I think nuclear is at some level unavoidable. When we think about what the energy mix will be for stationary power say 30 years from now or 40 years from now, it's very hard to see how you're going to avoid the use of nuclear power. **99**

—Robert Rosner, in *OnPoint*, "Argonne Lab Director Rosner Says Increasing Use of Nuclear Energy Unavoidable in U.S.," video, *E&ETV*, April 25, 2007. www.eenews.net.

Rosner is the director of the Argonne National Laboratory in Illinois.

Facts and Illustrations

Is Nuclear Power a Viable Energy Source?

- Today the United States operates **104 nuclear reactors**, of which 69 are pressurized water reactors and 35 are boiling water reactors.

- A typical nuclear power plant generates enough electricity each day to **power a city the size of Boston**.

- Between 7 and 10 tons (6.4 and 9.1 metric tons) of **natural uranium** are needed to generate 1 ton (0.91 metric tons) of **enriched uranium** suitable for use in most nuclear reactors.

- According to the International Atomic Energy Agency, reported uranium resources will last **83 years** at the current rate of consumption of 70,000 tons (63,503 metric tons) per year. By comparison, oil and gas reserves may be depleted in **30 to 50 years**.

- Each year, a typical nuclear power plant contributes up to **$20 million** to the state and local tax base and generates roughly **$75 million** in federal tax revenue.

- About **one-quarter** of nuclear production costs are related to the costs of the nuclear fuel uranium, which must be mined and processed into a form suitable for nuclear power production.

- Nuclear power plants operate in **31 U.S. states**. Vermont generates close to **80 percent** of its electricity from nuclear power. Other states in which nuclear power produces the largest share of electricity include New Jersey, South Carolina, Illinois, Connecticut, New Hampshire, and New York.

The Nuclear Power Plant

Nuclear reactors come in many designs, but basically work the same way to generate electricity at a nuclear power plant. This diagram shows a pressurized water reactor (PWR), the most widely used type of reactor in the world.

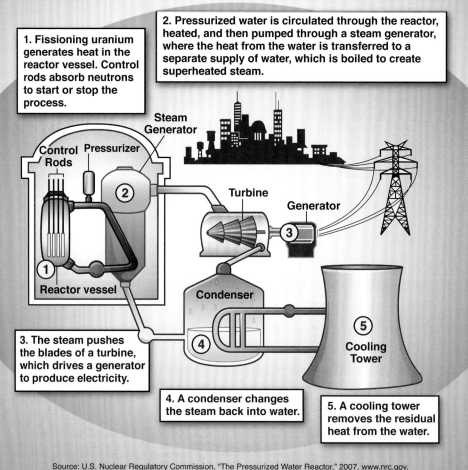

1. Fissioning uranium generates heat in the reactor vessel. Control rods absorb neutrons to start or stop the process.

2. Pressurized water is circulated through the reactor, heated, and then pumped through a steam generator, where the heat from the water is transferred to a separate supply of water, which is boiled to create superheated steam.

Steam Generator

Control Rods   Pressurizer

Turbine

Generator

②

①

Reactor vessel

Condenser

⑤

Cooling Tower

③

④

3. The steam pushes the blades of a turbine, which drives a generator to produce electricity.

4. A condenser changes the steam back into water.

5. A cooling tower removes the residual heat from the water.

Source: U.S. Nuclear Regulatory Commission, "The Pressurized Water Reactor," 2007. www.nrc.gov.

- On average, the construction of a new nuclear power plant will create **1,400 to 1,800 jobs.** Operation and maintenance of a plant generates an additional 400 to 700 full-time, permanent jobs.

Nuclear Share of Total Electricity Supply in 2008

Nuclear power provided close to 15 percent of the world's electricity supply in 2008. At least 15 countries used nuclear power to generate at least 25 percent of their electricity.

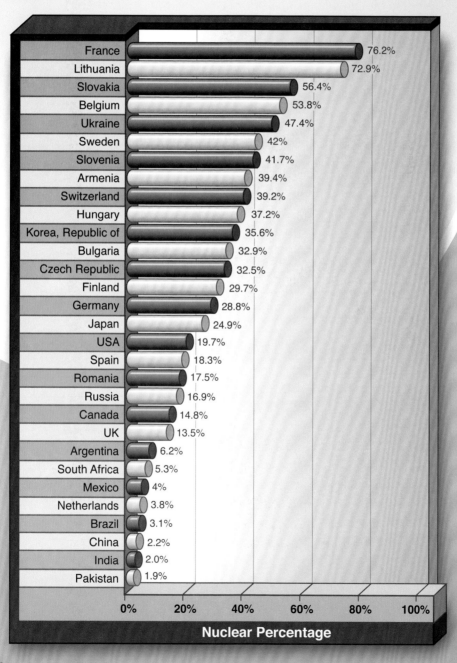

Country	Nuclear Percentage
France	76.2%
Lithuania	72.9%
Slovakia	56.4%
Belgium	53.8%
Ukraine	47.4%
Sweden	42%
Slovenia	41.7%
Armenia	39.4%
Switzerland	39.2%
Hungary	37.2%
Korea, Republic of	35.6%
Bulgaria	32.9%
Czech Republic	32.5%
Finland	29.7%
Germany	28.8%
Japan	24.9%
USA	19.7%
Spain	18.3%
Romania	17.5%
Russia	16.9%
Canada	14.8%
UK	13.5%
Argentina	6.2%
South Africa	5.3%
Mexico	4%
Netherlands	3.8%
Brazil	3.1%
China	2.2%
India	2.0%
Pakistan	1.9%

Nuclear Percentage

Source: International Atomic Energy Agency, "Nuclear Share of Total Electricity Generation in 2008," 2009. www.iaea.org.

Global Electricity Generation by Source

Fossil fuels—primarily coal, oil, and gas—generate the largest share of the electricity consumed in the world today. Here, thermal energy refers to electricity produced from coal, oil, gas, biomass, and waste. Renewable energy sources include geothermal, wind, solar, and tidal energy.

Country Group	Thermal	Hydro	Nuclear	Renewables
North America	66.15	13.72	19.04	1.09
Latin America	39.15	57.54	2.38	0.93
Western Europe	52.45	17.06	26.68	3.81
Eastern Europe	64.59	17.04	18.30	0.07
Africa	80.51	16.95	2.11	0.43
Middle East and South Asia	87.54	11.47	0.99	0.00
Southeast Asia and the Pacific	88.92	9.29		1.79
Far East	74.27	15.23	10.15	0.35
World Averages	**67.15**	**17.66**	**14.03**	**1.16**

Source: International Atomic Energy Agency, "Percentage Contribution of Each Fuel Type to Electricity Generation in 2008," 2009. www.iaea.org.

- Commercial uranium conversion plants—where uranium ore is chemically converted and enriched to a form usable as a **nuclear fuel**—operate in the United States, Canada, France, Russia, and the United Kingdom.

- Of the **30 countries** with nuclear power today, **6 intend to phase out their nuclear facilities** when current plants have reached the end of their life cycle.

U.S. Electricity Production Costs by Source, 1995–2008

The cost of producing electricity varies according to how the electricity is generated. In the graph, costs include plant operation and maintenance and fuel costs. A more in-depth breakdown of nuclear production costs includes indirect expenses, such as the cost to decommission a reactor, and investment costs, including the costs to construct or refurbish a nuclear power plant.

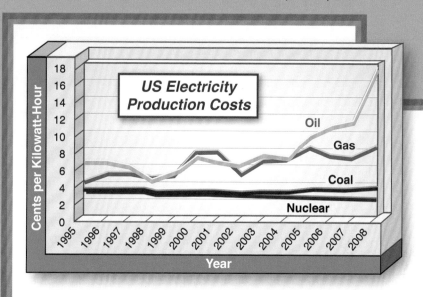

US Electricity Production Costs

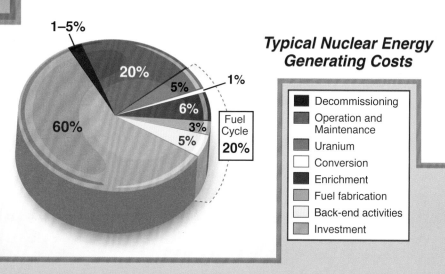

Typical Nuclear Energy Generating Costs

- Decommissioning
- Operation and Maintenance
- Uranium
- Conversion
- Enrichment
- Fuel fabrication
- Back-end activities
- Investment

Sources: Ventyx Velocity Suite and Nuclear Energy Institute/World Nuclear Association, "US Electricity Production Costs 1995–2008," 2009. www.world-nuclear.org; Nuclear Energy Association, "Nuclear Energy Today," 2007. www.nea.fr.

How Does Nuclear Power Affect the Environment?

66 Nuclear energy may just be the energy source that can save our planet from another possible disaster: catastrophic climate change. 99

—Patrick Moore, cofounder of Greenpeace and cochair of the Clean and Safe Energy Coalition.

66 Telling states to build new nuclear plants to combat global warming is like telling a patient to smoke to lose weight. 99

—Jennifer Nordstrom, coordinator of the Carbon-Free and Nuclear-Free campaign of the Institute for Energy and Environmental Research.

O ne of the most contentious environmental issues of the day is global warming. It refers to the average increase of global temperatures that contributes to changing climate patterns. To date, there is no consensus on the exact causes and consequences of this trend. Natural processes such as changes in the sun's intensity or volcanic eruptions, for example, can contribute to these changes, and indeed, the earth's climate has shifted between ice ages to periods of drought and warmth many times throughout history.

In recent years, however, human activities have played a more prominent role in changing the earth's atmosphere. Specifically, the combustion of fossil fuels—coal, oil, and gas—releases carbon dioxide (CO_2), one of the so-called greenhouse gases because it traps heat in the earth's atmosphere.

How Serious a Problem Is Global Warming?

Since the Industrial Revolution of the eighteenth and nineteenth centuries, the concentration of greenhouse gases in the atmosphere has increased dramatically, from 270 parts per million by volume to over 380 parts per million, and it continues to rise. The U.S. Environmental Protection Agency estimates that in 2007, the United States emitted over 7.7 billion tons (7 billion metric tons) of greenhouse gases. Up to three-quarters of these human-generated greenhouse gases are the by-product of the industrial processes that generate electricity.

While the precise effects of the changing composition of the earth's atmosphere are uncertain, most scientists concur that global warming is a pressing threat with potentially devastating implications. The Intergovernmental Panel on Climate Change, a scientific body established by the United Nations to assess climate change, has documented some of global warming's observable effects: "Warming of the climate system is unequivocal, as is now evident from observations of increases in global average air and ocean temperatures, widespread melting of snow and ice, and rising global average sea level."[15]

Can Nuclear Power Reduce Global Warming?

Many view climate change as one of the most important reasons for reconsidering the nation's current reliance on fossil fuels. As physicists Richard L. Garwin and Georges Charpak report in their book *Megawatts and Megatons: A Turning Point in the Nuclear Age?*: "If the level of carbon dioxide in the atmosphere (and its equivalent from other 'greenhouse gases') were to be held only to a doubling of the preindustrial level—i.e. that of 1850—more than half the world's energy would need to come from noncarbon sources by the year 2050."[16] In a similar vein, the International Atomic Energy Agency reported in 2008 that "in the absence of sweeping policy interventions, energy related CO_2 emissions are projected to increase by 55% in 2030 and by 130% in 2050."[17]

In light of these sober warnings, advocates believe that nuclear power can play a key role in decreasing greenhouse gas emissions, since nuclear plants, which generate electricity through fission, do not release CO_2

into the atmosphere. According to a 2008 report by the Nuclear Energy Institute: "By using nuclear energy rather than fossil fuel–based plants, electric utilities have prevented the release of 681 million metric tons of carbon dioxide emissions. For perspective, the volume of greenhouse gas emissions prevented at nuclear power plants is equivalent to taking 96 percent of all passenger cars off America's roadways."[18]

Even some environmentalists have joined the pro-nuclear movement, including Patrick Moore, one of the founders of Greenpeace. Moore, who supports a doubling of nuclear energy production, states, "Imagine if the ratio of coal to nuclear were reduced so that only 20 percent of our electricity was generated from coal and 60 percent from nuclear. This would go a long way toward cleaning the air and reducing greenhouse gas emissions. Every responsible environmentalist should support a move in that direction."[19]

> " **Many view climate change as one of the most important reasons for reconsidering the nation's current reliance on fossil fuels.** "

At the same time, many critics argue that nuclear power is not the answer to climate change for several reasons. While nuclear power produces virtually no CO_2 during electricity generation, enormous amounts of fossil fuels are burned during the entire nuclear fuel life cycle—from uranium mining to construction of nuclear power plants and the long-term storage of waste, for example. According to one study by the Intergovernmental Panel on Climate Change, the overall lifetime carbon emissions from a nuclear power plant may be similar to power plants that burn fossil fuels.

Furthermore, opponents charge, the industry continues to face myriad challenges that have prevented a nuclear renaissance for decades—problems with plant construction and licensing and prodigious costs, among other issues. A 2008 study by the Nuclear Information and Resource Service questions the feasibility of going nuclear to avert climate change: "New reactors would have to come online every few weeks for the next fifty years to have even a modest impact on GHG [greenhouse gas] emissions—new nuclear reactors cannot be built fast enough to address climate change."[20]

Nuclear Waste

There are several types of waste related to the nuclear fuel cycle. Low- and mid-level nuclear waste consists of tools, gloves, and other items used to handle radioactive materials and may come from laboratories, hospitals, or nuclear power facilities. These lower-level wastes are not very radioactive or long-lived and can be disposed of in shallow burial pits. Most high-level nuclear waste consists of spent nuclear fuel—that is, the reactor fuel that has reached a point where it no longer contributes to the nuclear chain reaction, although it remains radioactive for many centuries. The uranium-235 typically used in reactors, for example, has a half-life—the time it takes for half the nuclei in radioactive material to decay—of 10,000 years. The half-life of plutonium, another nuclear fuel, is closer to 25,000 years.

The storage containers and vaults that house the spent fuel rods must offer enough protection to prevent the toxic materials from seeping into the surrounding rocks, soil, rivers, and streams, which would expose people and animals to potentially dangerous levels of radiation. The spent fuel rods, along with the control rods and other products related to nuclear power generation, must be sequestered for tens of thousands of years. This is the time it takes for the radioactivity to decay to harmless levels, meaning to the level of natural background radiation which poses no threat to people or ecosystems. To put this into perspective, history only records the past several thousand years. As Michio Kaku and Jennifer Trainer comment in their book *Nuclear Power: Both Sides*: "The controversy surrounding waste boils down to one question: can we trust *any* man-made structure to isolate high-level waste for tens of thousands of years given our always-changing social institutions and the vagaries of war, revolutions, and social upheavals?"[21]

> " While nuclear power produces virtually no CO_2 during electricity generation, enormous amounts of fossil fuels are burned during the entire nuclear life cycle. "

Whether or not science can predict with certainty that these wastes can be prevented from entering the environment remains one of the most contentious issues related to nuclear power. At the same time, an increasing number of government officials and scientists believe that these challenges can and will be met and should not stymie the growth of an industry that can potentially alleviate global warming and address energy supply issues.

How Is Nuclear Waste Managed Today?

In comparison with fossil fuel combustion plants, the waste produced by commercial nuclear power plants is relatively small. For example, all of the waste ever produced by the nuclear industry in the United States would cover a football field about 5 yards (4.57m) deep. Put another way, according to journalist and nuclear proponent Gwyneth Cravens:

> The entire American inventory of waste presently being stored at nuclear power plants, after forty years of making trillions of kilowatt-hours of electricity and sparing the atmosphere billions of tons of carbon and greenhouse gases, comes to about fifty thousand metric tons. . . . By comparison, each year coal combustion in the United States alone yields one hundred million tons of ash and sludge containing toxic heavy metals.[22]

> **Whether or not science can predict with certainty that [nuclear] wastes can be prevented from entering the environment remains one of the most contentious issues related to nuclear power.**

The current U.S. policy is the direct deposit of waste in interim storage facilities. Today the roughly 2,200 tons (2,000 metric tons) of spent fuel produced each year is maintained near the reactor in which it was generated or an alternative site. It is typically submerged in pools of water to cool and then transferred to steel-reinforced dry casks.

These storage methods, however, are not intended for the long term; most scientists agree that nuclear waste should be permanently stored in steel containers in a deep, underground geological repository. To this end, Congress established the Nuclear Waste Policy Act in 1982. The act, which put a tax on electricity produced from nuclear power, has generated billions of dollars earmarked for the creation of a permanent repository for the nation's waste.

Yucca Mountain

Establishing a single, permanent nuclear waste site presents a number of technical challenges. Scientists must consider the possibility of geological events—seismic or volcanic activity, for example—that could rupture waste containers. Groundwater poses another problem, as water movement could erode the waste containers and carry the potentially lethal contents into the surrounding environment.

In 1987 Congress designated Yucca Mountain in Nevada for development as the nation's permanent waste repository. There scientists hoped to carve a maze of deep underground tunnels that could entomb up to 77 tons (70 metric tons) of waste for 10,000 years or more. Yucca Mountain appeared suitable for a number of reasons. Located in the remote desert approximately 90 miles (145km) northwest of Las Vegas, Yucca Mountain is extremely dry and far from any population center. Its geology, however, is extremely complex: Yucca Mountain

> " To reduce proliferation concerns . . . scientists hope to develop technologies to recycle nuclear fuels in ways that would render them unsuitable for nuclear weapons. "

rests on a fault line, although many geologists believe it to be inactive. The proximity of volcanoes—though dormant and likely to remain so for thousands of years to come—raises other concerns.

Potent political opposition and extensive legal wrangling have prevented final approval of the Yucca Mountain site. Opponents include antinuclear groups and key congressional leaders, most notably Nevada senator Harry Reid, the Senate majority leader, who has rallied against the facility since its inception. In 2009 the Yucca Mountain repository received a crushing blow when the Obama administration halted funding for the project. For now, the future of Yucca Mountain is uncertain. Although proponents continue in their attempts to keep the project alive, it will likely remain embroiled in controversy for years to come.

Reprocessing Nuclear Fuel

Another approach to nuclear waste management involves reprocessing spent fuel to extract the unused energy, which can then be reused to fuel a reactor. In essence, reprocessing chemically separates uranium and plutonium—a by-product of the nuclear fuel cycle—from other components in the waste. The remaining waste that requires permanent storage would be smaller in volume.

A primary objection to this approach is that the separated plutonium that can be used to fuel commercial reactors can also be used to make nuclear weapons. To prevent the military application of nuclear waste, U.S. president Jimmy Carter announced a ban on reprocessing in 1977. Reprocessing has been ongoing for years outside the United States, however. France, for example, has been reprocessing nuclear fuel since 1958. Today the Areva plant in La Hague on the French Cotentin Peninsula is the world's largest reprocessing plant, treating spent fuel that originates not only from within French borders, but also from Japan, Switzerland, the Netherlands, and other countries.

If reprocessing is to take hold in the United States, a number of issues must be addressed. To reduce proliferation concerns, for example, scientists hope to develop technologies to recycle nuclear fuels in ways that would render them unsuitable for nuclear weapons. Economic issues are also significant. The U.S. Department of Energy has estimated that a national reprocessing plant—which could process only half of all the waste generated domestically—could cost up to 20 billion dollars to construct. Many contend, too, that reprocessing is unnecessary because the nation's current policy of direct disposal is a secure option for years to come. These and other issues will likely generate wide debate—and drive public policy—in the future.

How Does Nuclear Power Affect the Environment?

❝ The attempt by the nuclear industry to anoint nuclear power as the solution to climate change is dangerous and threatens to squander the resources necessary to implement meaningful climate change mitigation policies. ❞

—Nuclear Information and Resource Service, "False Promises: Debunking Nuclear Industry Propaganda," May 2008. www.nirs.org.

The Nuclear Information and Resource Service is an information and networking center for individuals and organizations concerned about nuclear power and related issues.

❝ It is difficult to see how we can overcome climate change without nuclear energy being part of the solution. Nuclear power is green power. ❞

—Ralph Izzo, "A Green Nuclear Future," *Forbes*, September 21, 2007.

Izzo is the chair, president, and chief executive officer of the New Jersey–based Public Service Enterprise Group, one of the largest electric companies in the United States.

Bracketed quotes indicate conflicting positions.

* Editor's Note: While the definition of a primary source can be narrowly or broadly defined, for the purposes of Compact Research, a primary source consists of: 1) results of original research presented by an organization or researcher; 2) eyewitness accounts of events, personal experience, or work experience; 3) first-person editorials offering pundits' opinions; 4) government officials presenting political plans and/or policies; 5) representatives of organizations presenting testimony or policy.

66 **New nuclear generation, which has almost no carbon contribution and a tiny footprint on habitat, must be significantly increased.** 99

—The Boone and Crockett Club, "Climate Change Position Statement," August 2009. www.boone-crockett.org.

The Boone and Crockett Club is a conservationist organization founded by Theodore Roosevelt in 1887.

66 **The claim of the nuclear industry that nuclear power emits low levels of CO_2 and other greenhouse gases is not based on scientifically verifiable evidence.** 99

—Jan Willem Storm van Leeuwen, "Secure Energy? Civil Nuclear Power, Security, and Global Warming," Oxford Research Group, March 2007. www.oxfordresearchgroup.org.uk.

Storm van Leeuwen is a senior scientist at the Netherlands-based Ceedata Consultancy.

66 **[With reprocessing] it would be considerably more difficult to limit nuclear proliferation and to keep nuclear weapons out of the hands of terrorists desiring to commit mass murder on a horrific scale.** 99

—Al Gore, *Our Choice: A Plan to Solve the Climate Crisis.* Emmaus, PA: Rodale, 2009.

Al Gore is a former vice president of the United States and a long-standing environmental activist. Gore and the Intergovernmental Panel on Climate Change were jointly awarded the 2007 Nobel Peace Prize.

66 **As a nuclear engineer, I believe recycling holds great promise. With new reprocessing methods, it actually reduces the risk of nuclear proliferation.** 99

—Nolan Hertel, "State Should Tap Into Nuclear Recycling," *Atlanta Journal-Constitution*, February 7, 2007.

Hertel is a professor of nuclear and radiological engineering at Georgia Institute of Technology.

❝For every nuclear plant that environmentalists avoided, they ended up causing two coal plants to be built. . . . Most new power plants in this country are coal, because the environmentalists opposed nuclear.❞

—Vinod Khosla, "Five Questions for Vinod Khosla," interview with Katie Fehrenbacher, Earth2Tech, January 30, 2008. http://earth2tech.com.

Khosla is a cofounder of Sun Microsystems, a multinational vendor of computer software and information technology.

❝Monitoring and maintaining waste dumps over a period spanning 20 times the length of known civilization is an unacceptable burden to place on all future generations—with no guarantees of long-term safety.❞

—Greenpeace, "Climate Change—Nuclear Not the Answer," December 2007. www.greenpeace.org.

Greenpeace is a nongovernmental environmental advocacy organization that opposes nuclear power.

How Does Nuclear Power Affect the Environment?

- A typical nuclear power plant generates, on average, **22 tons** (20 metric tons) of nuclear waste each year. Overall, the U.S. nuclear industry generates about **2,200 tons** (2,000 metric tons) of waste per year.

- According to the Nuclear Energy Institute, improved efficiency and operating capacity at U.S. nuclear facilities represents a **one-third** reduction in the nation's industrial CO_2 emissions since 1993.

- Worldwide, nuclear-generated electricity prevents the release of about **2.75 billion tons** (2.5 billion metric tons) of CO_2 each year.

- Roughly **30 percent** of U.S. electricity comes from emission-free sources, of which nuclear power accounts for **70 percent**.

- The concept of a **shared international repository for radioactive waste**—in which a willing host country manages and stores the wastes from many countries—is currently under review by the European Repository Development Organisation.

- According to the Intergovernmental Panel on Climate Change, nuclear power had the largest potential to **mitigate climate change** out of the nine energy technologies assessed.

- Roughly **15 percent** of all spent fuel is reprocessed so that the uranium and plutonium can be reused. Reprocessing programs are underway in France, Japan, Russia, and the United Kingdom.

Emissions Avoided by Using Alternative Energy Sources in the United States, 2007

Fossil fuel combustion for electricity generation yields more greenhouse gas emissions, primarily carbon dioxide (CO_2), than renewable energy sources or nuclear power. The use of nuclear power in 2007 prevented the release of over 680 million metric tons of CO_2 into the atmosphere, had the electricity been generated by fossil fuel combustion.

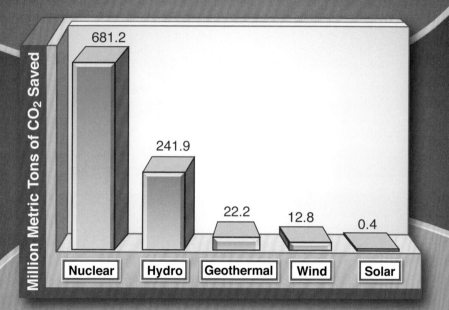

Source: Nuclear Energy Institute, "Nuclear Energy: Just the Facts," May 2008. www.nei.org.

- Each year, the global fleet of nuclear reactors generates approximately **12,000 tons** (10,886 metric tons) of spent fuel.

- Sweden, Finland, and France are currently developing **deep geological repositories** for spent nuclear fuel. These facilities will not be ready to accept waste before the year 2020.

- The reprocessing plant at La Hague, France, processes about **1,600 tons** (1,450 metric tons) of spent fuel each year.

Nuclear Waste in the United States

Nuclear-generated electricity produces thousands of tons of spent fuel that must be stored and managed for hundreds or even thousands of years. To offset the cost of the waste management, the Nuclear Waste Fund was established by Congress in 1982 so that those who use electricity supplied by nuclear power would pay for the used nuclear fuel disposal program. As of January 2009, 21 states have produced more than 1,000 metric tons of used nuclear fuel. Much of the revenue contributed to the waste fund was slated for the further development of Yucca Mountain, which President Obama put on hold in 2009.

State	Metric Tons of Uranium	Nuclear Waste Fund Contributions ($M)
Alabama	2,790	746.9
Arizona	1,710	528.6
Arkansas	1,180	295.6
California	2,590	819.3
Connecticut	1,890	364.1
Florida	2,720	766.1
Georgia	2,330	679.3
Illinois	7,420	1,777
Louisiana	1,080	321.1
Maryland	1,220	354.3
Michigan	2,310	524.5
Minnesota	1,090	386.2
New Jersey	2,280	597.9
New York	3,280	793.6
North Carolina	3,220	830
Pennsylvania	5,410	1,559.2
South Carolina	3,610	1,233.2
Tennessee	1,350	458.9
Texas	1,810	608.9
Virginia	2,240	691.8
Wisconsin	1,250	352.7

Source: ACI Nuclear Energy Solutions and Department of Energy/NEI, "U.S. State by State Commercial Nuclear Used Fuel and Payments to the Nuclear Waste Fund," July 2009. www.nei.org.

Is Nuclear Power Safe?

> ❝Opposition to nuclear power is based on irrational fear fed by Hollywood-style fiction, the Green lobbies, and the media. These fears are unjustified, and nuclear energy . . . has proved to be the safest of all energy sources.❞

—James Lovelock, British scientist, author, and environmentalist.

> ❝Nuclear power is an inherently dangerous activity. Splitting atoms is the most complicated and dangerous way to produce electricity.❞

—Jim Riccio, nuclear policy analyst for Greenpeace.

The principal risks associated with nuclear power arise from the adverse health effects linked to radiation exposure. To understand and quantify these risks, it is necessary to understand the properties of radiation.

Radiation

There are more than 100 types of atoms that make up all the matter in the universe. Some of these are unstable; they change spontaneously and emit invisible particles and energy waves called radiation. In fact, radiation occurs naturally in the environment and is everywhere; exposure, therefore, is inevitable. In the United States radiation doses are measured in units called REM. An average American receives a dose of about 360 millirem (one-thousandth of a REM) each year. Scientists estimate that a full 80 percent of a person's annual radiation exposure comes from the naturally occurring radiation in rocks, soil, radon gas, outer space, and similar sources. The remaining 20 percent comes from human-made sources such as diagnostic medical X-rays.

> **Excessive radiation exposure is associated with an increased risk of cancer and, to a lesser extent, an increased risk of genetic abnormalities that may transmit to the offspring of those exposed.**

Radiation can penetrate deep inside the human body and, at high levels, damage cells. A dose of 200 REM will cause radiation sickness, which can include vomiting, diarrhea, and fatigue. Higher doses cause burns on the skin. Degradation of the bone marrow, where red blood cells are produced, is a particularly lethal effect of radiation sickness. A dose of higher than 200 REM can cause death.

Damage can also appear months or even years after initial exposure. In particular, excessive radiation exposure is associated with an increased risk of cancer and, to a lesser extent, an increased risk of genetic abnormalities that may transmit to the offspring of those exposed. Epidemiological studies of more than 100,000 survivors of the atomic bombs unleashed on the Japanese cities Hiroshima and Nagasaki show that high levels of radiation were the likely cause of about 400 cancer deaths. While the risks associated with high doses of radiation are well established, the effects of low levels of exposure require more conclusive data.

Nuclear Reactors and Radioactive Release

A properly maintained and managed nuclear plant appears to release only a negligible amount of radiation into the environment. According to the U.S. Environmental Protection Agency, the naturally occurring gas radon found in the average American home exposes its occupants to a radiation dose of about 200 millirem annually. By way of comparison, a person living next to a nuclear power plant is exposed to less than 1 millirem of radiation over the course of a year. Put another way, Americans receive 0.1 percent of their total annual radiation exposure from nuclear activities. They receive 5 times that amount from gases released into the atmosphere during coal-fired electricity generation.

An accident at a nuclear power plant could result in the unintended release of radiation into the atmosphere, however, and safety measures are necessarily stringent. A particular concern is that the heat produced in a reactor could overcome the cooling system's ability to stabilize temperatures. An extreme system failure could result in nuclear meltdown— that is, the nuclear material could potentially "melt" right through the containment vessel and blast dangerous quantities of radioactive steam and debris into the surrounding environment. According to Jim Riccio of Greenpeace, "If a meltdown were to occur . . . the accident could kill and injure tens of thousands of people, cost billions of dollars in damages, and leave large regions uninhabitable."[23]

On the other hand, nuclear advocates insist that the precautions that prevent such an event are effective. Extensive safety measures and backup systems exist to monitor and prevent every conceivable problem that could compromise a reactor, including human error, equipment failure, acts of terrorism,

> " **Data on the long-term effects of radiation exposure are inconclusive, but the World Health Organization estimated that close to 10,000 people died or will die of cancer related to Chernobyl.** "

and natural disasters such as earthquakes and tornadoes. Fuel pellets, for example, are encased in ceramic and then placed in zirconium fuel rods that prevent them from overheating, and a redundancy of control rods, which stop the fission process, are ready to slow down or stop the chain reaction. Reactors, too, are designed so that an increased level of steam causes the nuclear reaction to slow down or stop completely, and emergency cooling systems are designed to inject water into the reactor core should it overheat. Finally, a steel pressure vessel and thick concrete dome that cover the reactor prevent radioactivity from leaking into the environment.

These multiple safety systems are called "defense in depth." The former chair of the U.S. Nuclear Regulatory Commission, Nils Diaz, described this approach:

It is really more than a philosophy: it is an action plan, an approach to ensuring protection. The concept of "defense-in-depth" is a centerpiece of our approach to ensuring public health and safety, and it goes beyond pieces of equipment. It calls for, among other things, high quality design, fabrication, construction, inspection, and testing; plus multiple barriers to fission product release; plus redundancy and diversity in safety equipment; plus procedures and strategies; and lastly, emergency preparedness.[24]

Natural Disasters and Terrorist Attacks

The defense-in-depth approach addresses the many unexpected contingencies that could damage or weaken a reactor core. Reactors in earthquake prone areas, for example, have automatic shutoff systems that activate when sensors detect seismic movement. Recent earthquakes in Japan, for example, are testament to the effectiveness of these systems. When a large quake rattled Japan's Kashiwazaki-Kariwa nuclear plant in July 2007, the physical structure withstood the seismic activity, and all safety systems—including the automatic shutdown feature—deployed as designed, according to an assessment by the International Atomic Energy Agency.

The threat of terrorism must also be managed. Indeed, the attacks on the World Trade Center and the Pentagon on September 11, 2001, escalated fears that the nation's nuclear power plants could be targeted by al Qaeda or other terrorist groups. Although a terrorist attack could take many forms, experts generally focus on airplane suicide attacks or the possibility of a terrorist detonating a bomb in or near the reactor core. A compromised reactor would not only interrupt the nation's electricity supply, but could also release highly radioactive material into the atmosphere. According to one disaster scenario presented by the Union of Concerned Scientists, an attack that breached the reactor of the Indian Point plant in New York could result in 44,000 immediate deaths from radiation sickness and up to 500,000 long-term deaths from cancer among individuals exposed to the radiation.

At present, it remains debatable just how vulnerable the nation's nuclear facilities are to terrorist attacks. In the view of Physicians for Social Responsibility, a group that opposes nuclear power: "Nuclear reactors are not designed to withstand attacks using large aircraft, such as those used on September 11, 2001. A well-coordinated attack could have severe consequences for human health and the environment."[25]

Others counter that the structures that protect the reactor core are extremely robust—among the most impenetrable ever built—and are indeed capable of withstanding attacks similar to those of September 11. Referring to the nuclear-powered sea vessels that have been operating for years with little incident, Peter W. Huber and Mark P. Mills state: "The U.S. Navy sails nuclear reactors around the globe in steel ships; protecting land-based civilian plants presents a comparatively trivial engineering challenge."[26] A study by the Electric Power Research Institute appears to support this view, concluding that nuclear reactors could indeed withstand the impact of a large commercial aircraft or similar attack. While the level of threat posed by terrorist activity remains unquantifiable, human error played the primary role in two of the worst nuclear accidents to date.

> " **Both nuclear bombs and nuclear reactors are based on the same technology and raw ingredients.** "

Lessons Learned from Three Mile Island and Chernobyl

Many lessons were learned from the accidents at Three Mile Island in 1979 and Chernobyl in 1986. At Three Mile Island, a malfunctioning water pump caused a series of events that led the reactor operators, who did not understand what was happening, to shut down the main coolant pumps. The reactor vessel got so hot that the fuel rods melted. The coolant flow was ultimately restored, and the containment vessel prevented the release of radioactive materials from the crippled reactor core. In response to the accident, the U.S. nuclear industry launched two investigatory commissions, which led to the creation of the Institute of Nuclear Power Operations. This agency sets standards within the nuclear industry and rates the performance of individual plants. It also trains and evaluates reactor operators and conducts emergency preparedness exercises.

The Chernobyl meltdown was also driven by human error—the crew of operators disabled the reactor's automatic shutdown mechanism as part of an equipment safety test. At the same time, there were significant flaws in the plant design. A deficient cooling system led to an uncontrolled chain reaction and sent temperatures skyrocketing, and an insufficient containment vessel—it was not fully enclosed—did not contain the explosion that followed. Thirty-one people died immediately, and many more died in the months and years following the disaster. Data on the long-term effects of radiation exposure are inconclusive, but the World Health Organization estimated that close to 10,000 people died or will die of cancer related to Chernobyl. Greenpeace International and other organizations have put death toll figures much higher.

> **The situation in Iran and other unstable regions of the world suggests to many that the provisions of the Nuclear Nonproliferation Treaty and the International Atomic Energy Agency must be broadened.**

The defects in the Soviet-designed reactor contrast sharply with western designs and have since been modified in all Soviet reactors since Chernobyl. At the same time, the nuclear industry established the World Association of Nuclear Operators, an international body that performs a function similar to the Institute of Nuclear Power Operations. Today every organization that operates an electricity-generating nuclear plant is a member of the World Association of Nuclear Operators. In light of such industry changes, many believe that another Chernobyl-type meltdown is highly unlikely.

Nuclear Proliferation

Both nuclear bombs and nuclear reactors are based on the same technology and raw ingredients—that is, an enriched form of uranium or plutonium. When these fissile materials are used to produce electricity, however, they produce a chain reaction that is slow and controlled. In nuclear weapons, the uranium is enriched from about 4 percent to a highly fissile 90 percent, and the chain reaction is left uncontrolled, producing an explosion so immense that it can flatten cities and spread radioactive gas and debris over entire continents.

With such high stakes, a variety of measures exist to control nuclear proliferation—the spread of nuclear weapons and, specifically, the materials and technologies necessary to build them. Established in 1968, the Nuclear Nonproliferation Treaty (NPT) is an international treaty to prevent the spread of nuclear weapons. At present, 189 countries have signed the treaty, including the five countries recognized by the agreement as nuclear states: China, France, Russia, the United Kingdom, and the United States. Nations that have not signed the treaty include India, Pakistan, North Korea, and Israel, although these countries have significant nuclear programs. Signatories agree to safeguard their nuclear materials and facilities and to undergo regular inspections by the International Atomic Energy Agency, among other provisions. In addition, nonnuclear states agree to forgo the military use of nuclear power in exchange for the technology to develop it for electricity generation.

Many feel that the safeguard system under the Nuclear Nonproliferation Treaty has been successful in halting the diversion of civil uranium for military applications. At the same time, the treaty's safeguards are limited. The risk that a nation will disregard the provisions of the treaty is very real, and numerous examples bear this out. Iran, for example, has secretly attempted to enrich uranium even after agreeing to the treaty's provisions against doing so, and many experts remain deeply concerned over Iran's intentions.

> **A variety of measures exist to control nuclear proliferation— the spread of nuclear weapons.**

The situation in Iran and other unstable regions of the world suggests to many that the provisions of the Nuclear Nonproliferation Treaty and the International Atomic Energy Agency must be broadened. Nuclear opponents go further, charging that as long as civilian nuclear power plants continue to operate, the technology and materials could be diverted to terrorist groups and rogue states hostile to the United States and other countries—or even used as a guise for weapons development. As former vice president Al Gore writes:

During the eight years I worked in the White House, every nuclear weapons–proliferation problem we faced was connected to a reactor program. . . . A team of scientists and engineers capable of managing a nuclear reactor program and at least part of the nuclear fuel cycle can be forced by a dictator to work secretly on a nuclear weapons program. Indeed, that is the principal way nuclear weapons have proliferated in the last 25 years.[27]

Whether the international community will be able to persuade all nations to use nuclear technology solely for peaceful purposes—and whether the fission reaction can be safely managed when used in this context—will be determined in the years ahead.

Is Nuclear Power Safe?

> **Existing plants are safe and efficient, and the next generation promises to be more passively safe and more efficient.**

—John Rowe, "America's Energy Future: Carbon, Competition, and Kilowatts," speech at the Brookings Institution, February 12, 2008. www.brookings.edu.

Rowe is the chair, president, and chief executive officer of Exelon, one of the largest electric utilities—and nuclear operators—in the nation.

....

> **Each nuclear reactor has the potential to devastate the region in which it operates.**

—Jim Riccio, "Risky Business: The Probability and Consequences of a Nuclear Accident," Greenpeace report, March 14, 2008. www.greenpeace.org.

Riccio is a nuclear policy analyst for Greenpeace.

....

Bracketed quotes indicate conflicting positions.

* Editor's Note: While the definition of a primary source can be narrowly or broadly defined, for the purposes of Compact Research, a primary source consists of: 1) results of original research presented by an organization or researcher; 2) eyewitness accounts of events, personal experience, or work experience; 3) first-person editorials offering pundits' opinions; 4) government officials presenting political plans and/or policies; 5) representatives of organizations presenting testimony or policy.

66While the United States has one of the world's most well-developed regulatory systems for protecting nuclear facilities against sabotage and attack, today's security standards are inadequate to defend against credible threats.99

—Union of Concerned Scientists, "Nuclear Power in a Warming World: Assessing the Risks, Addressing the Challenges," December 2007. www.ucsusa.org.

The Union of Concerned Scientists is a nonprofit partnership of scientists and citizens working to achieve practical solutions to environmental problems.

66The commission is confident that nuclear power plants . . . continue to be among the best-protected private sector facilities in the nation.99

—U.S. Nuclear Regulatory Commission, "Report to Congress on the Security Inspections Program for Commercial Power Reactor and Cat 1 Fuel Cycle Facilities: Results and Status Update," 2008. www.nrc.gov.

The U.S. Nuclear Regulatory Commission was created by Congress in 1974 to regulate commercial nuclear power plants and other uses of nuclear materials.

66Everybody thinks of Three Mile Island as some kind of terrible disaster. It was a bad mechanical failure that cost a lot of money. But no member of the public was injured.99

—Patrick Moore, interview with Tucker Carlson, *Tucker*, MSNBC, November 9, 2007. www.msnbc.msn.com.

Moore is a cofounder of Greenpeace and cochair of the Clean and Safe Energy Coalition.

66The actual levels of radiation released into the surrounding areas [of the Three Mile Island reactor], as reported by the government, may be . . . as much as 1,000 times [higher than reported].99

—Concerned Citizens for Nuclear Safety, "New Three Mile Island Information Provides Warning for Future," April 10, 2009. www.nuclearactive.org.

Concerned Citizens for Nuclear Safety is a nonprofit organization that researches and disseminates information on a wide range of nuclear safety issues.

66 If nuclear power were really as dangerous as people believe, isn't France—with its 59 nuclear reactors making 78% of its power—grossly polluted and doomed? Far from it. **99**

—James Lovelock, "Our Nuclear Lifeline," *Reader's Digest*, March 2005.

Lovelock is a British scientist, author, and environmentalist. In the United States Lovelock has taught at Yale University and Harvard University.

....

66 [If] nuclear power [becomes] the silver-bullet option of choice for electricity production, thousands of additional reactors would be built. And many of them would be placed in countries that most people would agree should not possess nuclear weapons. **99**

—Al Gore, *Our Choice: A Plan to Solve the Climate Crisis*. Emmaus, PA: Rodale, 2009.

Al Gore is a former vice president of the United States and a long-standing environmental activist. Gore and the Intergovernmental Panel on Climate Change were jointly awarded the 2007 Nobel Peace Prize.

....

Facts and Illustrations

Is Nuclear Power Safe?

- The 1979 motion picture *The China Syndrome*, which fictionalized a catastrophic nuclear meltdown scenario, helped galvanize public opposition to nuclear power. The film's title became a catchphrase for antinuclear activists.

- Over the past 40 years, more than **3,000 shipments** of high-level nuclear waste contained in reinforced shipping containers have been transported by rail, highway, and occasionally waterway—with **no release of radioactive material**.

- Although fabrication of nuclear components—vessels, valves, pumps, electronics, etc.—takes place at numerous locations, all construction is performed under the regulatory scrutiny of the **U.S. Nuclear Regulatory Commission**.

- In January 2009, 110 nuclear safety experts from 40 countries participated in the International Meeting on Environmental Modeling for Radiation Safety to assess **radiation risks** related to uranium mining and nuclear plant operations and to review and update safety guidelines.

- In 12,000 cumulative reactor years of commercial nuclear power plant operation in 30 countries, only **two major accidents** have occurred, at Chernobyl and Three Mile Island.

Sources of Radiation Exposure in the United States

Radiation is typically measured in units called millirem (mrem). According to the American Nuclear Society, humans are exposed, on average, to about 360 mrem per year, although some people are exposed to much higher levels. For comparison, living within 50 miles of a nuclear power plant adds roughly .01 mrem per year.

Annual Dose in Mrem

Radiation Source	Radiation Amount (mrem per year)
Cigarette smoking (1 pack per day)	1,300
Radon in homes	200
Medical X-rays and pharmaceuticals	53
Direct exposure from naturally occurring radioactivity in soil	30
Cosmic radiation	30
Continental round trip air travel	5
Building materials	3.6

Percent of Total Radiation Dose by Source

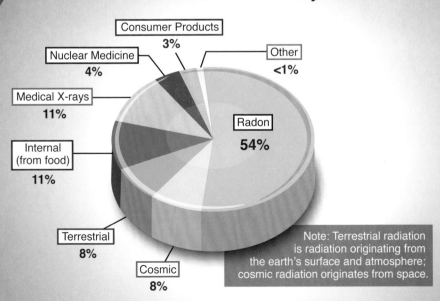

Consumer Products 3%

Other <1%

Nuclear Medicine 4%

Medical X-rays 11%

Internal (from food) 11%

Radon 54%

Terrestrial 8%

Cosmic 8%

Note: Terrestrial radiation is radiation originating from the earth's surface and atmosphere; cosmic radiation originates from space.

Source: Farmingdale State College/Mechanical Engineering Department, "Sources of Radiation Exposure to the U.S. Population," January 2007.

61

Industrial Accident Rate Relatively Low at U.S. Nuclear Power Plants

Operational safety at nuclear power plants is one way to measure overall safety of the nuclear industry, since an accident at a nuclear plant could dramatically impact public health and safety. In the United States, there has been only one major nuclear accident, which occurred at the Three Mile Island facility in Pennsylvania in 1979. Since then, all other incidents have been completely confined to the nuclear plant. Here, the industrial safety accident rate refers to the number of accidents resulting in lost work, restricted work, or fatalities for every 200,000 person-hours worked in a given year.

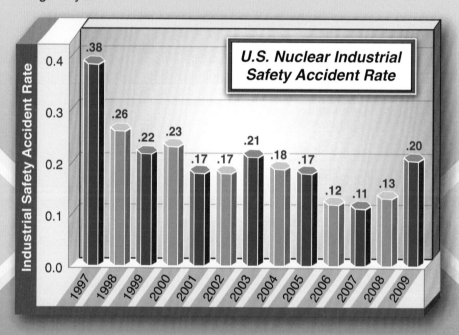

Source: Nuclear Energy Institute/World Nuclear Association, "U.S. Nuclear Industrial Safety Accident Rate," April 2009. www.world-nuclear.org.

- The International Atomic Energy Agency and other organizations have proposed the creation of a **multinational nuclear fuel bank**, which would ensure a secure and reliable supply of fuel and strengthen non-proliferation efforts through a system of safeguards and oversight.

Nuclear Reactor Containment Structures

Nuclear reactors are designed with multiple layers of safety. In addition to extensive safety procedures and controls, such as automated systems, myriad physical barriers prevent the release of radiation from the reactor core that houses the fissionable materials.

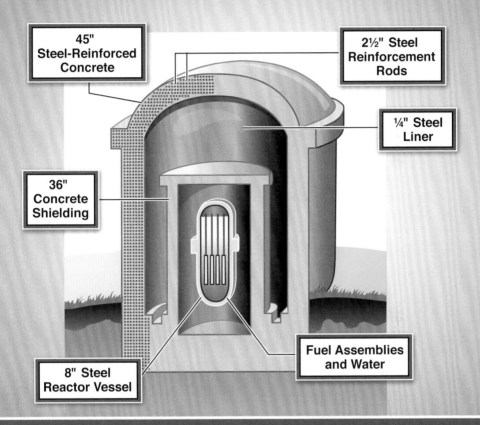

45" Steel-Reinforced Concrete

2½" Steel Reinforcement Rods

¼" Steel Liner

36" Concrete Shielding

8" Steel Reactor Vessel

Fuel Assemblies and Water

Source: Nuclear Energy Institute, "Nuclear Power: Just the Facts," May 2008. www.nei.org.

- Between January and June 2009, the International Atomic Energy Agency's Illicit Trafficking Database received reports of **215 incidents** of unauthorized possession and trafficking of nuclear materials.

- Over **50 percent** of the nation's nuclear power plants are in close proximity to large metropolitan areas, including Washington, D.C., and New York City.

What Is the Future of Nuclear Power?

❝The [nuclear] industry remains moribund in the United States, and its worldwide growth has slowed dramatically.❞

—Al Gore, forty-fifth vice president of the United States and an environmental activist.

❝There will be substantial growth in nuclear power use in the world in the coming decades, a non-polluting form of power spurring economic development.❞

—Michael Corradini, engineering physics chair at the University of Wisconsin at Madison.

There has been a paucity of new reactor construction in the United States for the last several decades. However, the strategies to develop nuclear power continue to evolve—domestically and internationally—as scientists seek novel approaches to obtaining a sustainable energy future.

Next Generation Nuclear Reactors

Nuclear designs are divided into four categories. Generation I refers to early prototype reactors, Generation II and III to the nuclear plants that are being designed or are in operation around the world today, and Generation IV to the systems that will be designed and built in the decades ahead. The Generation IV program aims to develop nuclear systems that will advance the safety and reliability of reactors and use fuel more efficiently, thereby minimizing waste and proliferation risks.

The Generation IV International Forum formed in 2001 to expand nuclear research and development through the collaborative efforts of nuclear nations. The forum has 13 members, including Canada, France, Japan, the United States, the United Kingdom, China, and Russia. The Generation IV International Forum and other groups hope to introduce the next generation systems between 2015 and 2030.

Other measures support these next generation programs. For example, the U.S. Department of Energy announced in September 2009 that it would finance up to $40 million for the development of these future reactors. At an Energy Department conference the same year, the organization emphasized the role universities must play in educating the nuclear engineers of tomorrow. These efforts will help ensure that the United States has sufficient technical expertise to maintain its current nuclear fleet and to support the next generation nuclear system designs. Supporters of nuclear power hope that these and other initiatives will play a vital role in expanding the now-stagnant nuclear power industry in the United States. As Senator Pete Domenici comments on the current status of the domestic nuclear program:

> The first step toward a sustainable energy plan is a commitment to rejuvenate nuclear power's future by reversing the quarter-century dearth of new plant construction. We simply must see new domestic plants constructed. It does us little good to compliment ourselves on our foresight in developing and licensing advanced reactor designs— U.S. designs that are providing reliable power elsewhere in the world today—when we have none of these reactor designs under construction here.[28]

New Reactor Designs

Scientists are exploring a variety of new designs—over 100—to further the goals of the Generation IV initiative. One design that offers significant advantages over current systems is the pebble bed modular reactor, a gas-cooled reactor that operates at high temperatures and uses over 350,000 spherical fuel pebbles instead of the fuel rods that power today's reactors. The novel packaging of fuel in the pebble bed system dramatically enhances safety. Each pebble of uranium oxide is encased in a graphite shell that can withstand exceedingly high temperatures. Thus, even if the cooling system fails and the temperature in the reactor core rises to unsafe levels, the pebbles would be unlikely to catch fire or melt. That the system is able to operate at such high temperatures enhances efficiency as well. Today various forms of the pebble bed reactor are under development. So far, China has the world's only pebble bed reactor prototype in operation, although South Africa has announced plans to build a pebble bed system in coming years.

> "The Generation IV program aims to develop nuclear systems that will advance the safety and reliability of reactors and use fuel more efficiently."

The International Reactor Innovative and Secure is another promising system. Designed by Westinghouse, this water-cooled reactor incorporates a number of features that ensure that the primary system does not suffer a loss of coolant. The entire cooling system, for example, is housed inside a fortified pressure vessel, in contrast to current systems that typically pump the coolant into the core. Moreover, the cooling system relies on gravity and other natural forces instead of pumps, fans, and other machinery that can malfunction. These simplified operating systems present far fewer opportunities for technical problems to occur. The design is also smaller—and potentially more cost competitive—than reactors in operation today.

Breeder Reactors

Another type of reactor, the breeder reactor, is unique in that it creates more fuel than it consumes and generates less high-level waste than traditional reactors. The fast breeder, a type of breeder reactor, uses a mixture of uranium and plutonium as fuel. Unlike uranium, plutonium does not require slow neutrons to undergo fission, so moderators, which are required to slow uranium atoms to a speed suitable for fission, are unnecessary. Besides using "fast" neutrons, these specialized reactors produce, or "breed," more fuel by converting uranium into plutonium, which can be put back in the reactor and reused to fuel the fission process.

Experimental breeder reactors have operated in several countries. These prototypes have had only limited success, however. They are extremely difficult to build and expensive to operate, and most have been decommissioned. The world's first breeder reactor came online in Idaho in 1951 and produced, for the first time, nuclear-powered electricity. Intended for research purposes only, this first breeder reactor was never used commercially. France's first fast breeder, the Superphénix, began producing electricity in 1986, although it was permanently shut down during the 1990s. Likewise, fast breeders in Scotland and Japan have also been decommissioned, as they suffered technical difficulties and were not economically feasible.

Another concern with breeder reactors is that the plutonium produced could be diverted for weapons use. Whether these reactors can be made economical to run and operate—and whether the plutonium produced can be safely managed—will determine the long-term fate of the breeder program. Today international interest in breeder reactor technology continues despite these challenges. China, Japan, India, Korea, and Russia are among the countries that have announced plans to pursue breeder technology.

> " One design that offers significant advantages over current systems is the pebble bed modular reactor, a gas-cooled reactor that operates at high temperatures and uses over 350,000 spherical fuel pebbles. "

In the United States GE-Hitachi is currently developing a fast breeder reactor called the Prism. It is designed to extract the unused energy from the spent fuel rods already sitting in nuclear storage sites across the country. Similarly, General Atomics, a nuclear and defense contractor, made public its plans to design a new kind of compact commercial nuclear reactor in February 2010. Like the Prism, the Energy Multiplier Module, or EM2, could run on the nation's stockpile of spent nuclear fuel. In addition to tapping the energy in existing waste and thereby reducing its volume and toxicity, the EM2 design has other unique features. For instance, the EM2 would be about

60 feet (18m) long and 16 feet (4.9m) in diameter—about one-quarter the size of most current reactors. These smaller reactors would be far easier to manufacture and transport, which could push down the generally exorbitant production costs of new reactor construction. The EM2 would also run at exceedingly high temperatures, making it extremely efficient and suitable for industrial processes other than energy production. While the research for these prototypes is underway, it will likely require years to perfect the novel designs and to secure the funding and licensing necessary to bring them online.

Is Fusion the Future?

The world of the future could be powered by the energy from nuclear fusion—the same process that takes place in the sun and other stars. A nuclear reactor powered by fusion would work in an entirely different way from the fission reactors of today. During fusion—the exact opposite of fission—the nuclei of two atoms join, or fuse, together to form a larger nucleus. This joining creates immense energy.

Fusion has the potential to produce the enormous energy required by the post-industrial world in the century ahead. In addition, the fuel used to produce a fusion reaction is not radioactive, nor does it produce radioactive waste, as do the uranium and plutonium that fuel the fission process. In experiments to create power by fusion, rather, scientists aim to fuse isotopes of hydrogen called deuterium, which comes from water, and tritium, which can be made from the metal lithium in the earth's crust.

> **Fusion has the potential to produce the enormous energy required by the post-industrial world in the century ahead.**

At the same time, fusion presents daunting scientific challenges. To create a fusion reaction—to cause the nuclei to crash into each other and fuse—requires temperatures of millions of degrees—hotter, even, than the sun. Such extreme temperatures will destroy almost anything that contains it. As Russ Doerner, a research scientist studying fusion at the University of California at San Diego, put it: "With . . . fusion you are basically trying to build a sun on earth. But you have to put the sun inside of something. The sun tries to melt walls."[29]

The Tokamak

In 1970 scientists in the former Soviet Union designed a doughnut-shaped magnetic chamber, called a tokamak, to hold the immense heat required to create a fusion reaction. Since then the tokamak has become the primary design in fusion research. Today several of these experimental fusion reactors are in operation. For example, the Joint European Torus in Culham, England, began operating in 1983. In its characteristic doughnut-shaped reactor, fuel is held in place by powerful magnets as it is heated to over 180 million degrees Fahrenheit (100 million degrees Celsius). At these super-hot temperatures, the fuel's electrons leave the nuclei, creating a hot, electrically charged gas known as a plasma. These incredibly hot plasmas create the environment in which elements can fuse together and produce energy. To create the plasma, however, requires an enormous amount of energy—far more energy than the reaction produces. This is true at all existing fusion facilities so far.

> **The deployment of a large-scale nuclear program depends on how well science can address the challenging issues regarding economic viability, operational safety, waste management, and weapons nonproliferation.**

In 2006 the United States joined with China, the European Union, India, Japan, Korea, and Russia in signing an agreement to construct an international fusion research facility in Cadarache, France. Known as ITER (formerly the International Thermonuclear Experimental Reactor), the goal of the project is to build a tokamak that will produce more power than it consumes—and ultimately demonstrate the feasibility of energy produced from fusion. According to ITER's Web site: "Fusion has the potential to play an important role as part of a future energy mix for our planet. It has the capacity to produce energy on a large scale, using plentiful fuels, and releasing no carbon dioxide or other greenhouse gases. ITER is an important step on the road to fusion power plants."[30]

Currently, construction on ITER is underway, and steady progress continues at other test fusion facilities, including Princeton Plasma Physics Laboratory in New Jersey and Sandia National Laboratory in New Mexico. With so many challenges to overcome, however, electricity produced from fusion is likely decades away.

A Nuclear Renaissance?

In recent years the U.S. nuclear industry has put forth efforts to build public support for a "nuclear renaissance." For example, as part of a recent campaign, the Nuclear Energy Institute has disseminated close to 100 print ads promoting nuclear power as a clean, secure energy source. Along with the growing threat of global warming, dwindling fuel supplies, and increasing reluctance to depend on potentially hostile foreign sources for energy, these efforts may be fostering greater public acceptance of nuclear power. Several studies bear this out. Recent public opinion polls by the Nuclear Energy Institute, the Gallup organization, and others show a sharp increase in public acceptance since the days following the Chernobyl accident.

The deployment of a large-scale nuclear program depends on how well science can address the challenging issues regarding economic viability, operational safety, waste management, and weapons nonproliferation. At the same time, the human demand for energy is rising dramatically. As authors Peter W. Huber and Mark P. Mills write in their book *The Bottomless Well*:

> The demand for electricity has been rising without interruption since Edison invented the light bulb over a century ago. Short of some massive economic convulsion that drastically shrinks the economy it will go on rising. . . . Economic growth marches hand in hand with increased consumption of electricity—always, everywhere, without significant exception in the annals of modern industrial history.[31]

There is scant debate that the developed world—and emerging economies—will require an increasingly large and diverse supply of energy. How these energy demands will be met and what role nuclear power will play will be determined in the years to come.

What Is the Future of Nuclear Power?

66 **The nuclear industry is promoting a new generation of reactors. However, these are relatively untested and far from proven.** 99

—Greenpeace, "Climate Change: Nuclear Not the Answer," 2009. www.greenpeace.org.

Greenpeace is a nongovernmental environmental advocacy organization that stands in opposition to nuclear energy.

66 **It's time to stop running scared from Chernobyl and start realizing that we now have the systems and technology to build fail-safe nuclear power plants.** 99

—Lee Iacocca, *Where Have All the Leaders Gone?* New York: Scribner's, 2007.

Iacocca is the former president and chief executive officer of the Chrysler Corporation.

Bracketed quotes indicate conflicting positions.

* Editor's Note: While the definition of a primary source can be narrowly or broadly defined, for the purposes of Compact Research, a primary source consists of: 1) results of original research presented by an organization or researcher; 2) eyewitness accounts of events, personal experience, or work experience; 3) first-person editorials offering pundits' opinions; 4) government officials presenting political plans and/or policies; 5) representatives of organizations presenting testimony or policy.

66 **Nuclear power is continuing its decades-long collapse in the global marketplace because it's grossly uncompetitive, unneeded, and obsolete.** 99

—Amory Lovins and Imran Sheikh, "The Nuclear Illusion," Rocky Mountain Institute, May 27, 2008. www.rmi.org.

Lovins is a physicist and cofounder of the Rocky Mountain Institute. Sheikh is a graduate student at the University of California at Berkeley.

66 **Nuclear energy is one of the few bright spots in the U.S. economy—expanding rather than contracting, and creating thousands of jobs over the past few years.** 99

—Scott Peterson, in Nuclear Energy Institute, "Statement by Scott Peterson, Vice President, Nuclear Energy Institute, Washington, D.C.," May 28, 2009. www.nei.org.

Peterson is the vice president of the Nuclear Energy Institute, the policy organization of the nuclear energy and technologies industry.

66 **A worldwide nuclear 'renaissance' is beyond the capacity of the nuclear industry to deliver, and would stretch to breaking point the capacity of the [International Atomic Energy Agency] to monitor and safeguard civil nuclear power.** 99

—Frank Barnaby and James Kemp, *Too Hot To Handle: The Future of Civil Nuclear Power*. London: Oxford Research Group, 2007.

Barnaby is a nuclear issues consultant at Oxford Research Group, a UK-based organization that promotes nonmilitary resolutions to global conflict. Kemp is a research associate at the organization.

66 **We must harness the power of nuclear energy on behalf of our efforts to combat climate change, and to advance peace and opportunity to all people.** 99

—Barack Obama, "Remarks by President Barack Obama," speech in Prague, Czech Republic, April 5, 2009. www.whitehouse.gov.

Obama is the forty-fourth president of the United States.

66 In the coming decades, we will have to convert to solar power and safe nuclear power, both of which offer essentially unbounded energy supplies. 99

—Jeffrey Sachs, "Are Malthus's Predicted 1798 Food Shortages Coming True?" *Scientific American*, September 2008. www.scientificamerican.com.

Sachs is the director of the Earth Institute at Columbia University.

66 The perfect energy source is one that doesn't take up much space, has a virtual inexhaustible supply, is safe, doesn't put any carbon into the atmosphere, doesn't leave any long lived radioactive waste; it's fusion. 99

—Stephen Cowley, "Fusion Is Energy's Future," speech, TEDGlobal, July 2009. www.TED.com.

Cowley is the director of the Culham Fusion Science Center in the United Kingdom.

66 Harnessing the potential of existing low-carbon technologies is crucial: Only by making the decision early to invest will countries be able to benefit from the next generation of nuclear energy. 99

—Nicholas Stern, "Key Elements of a Global Deal on Climate Change," report, London School of Economics and Political Science, May 30, 2008.

Stern is an economist and I.G. Patel Chair in Economics and Government at the London School of Economics and Political Science.

What Is the Future of Nuclear Power?

- Most of the world's operating reactors are based on **second-generation designs** from the late 1960s and 1970s. The world's first third-generation nuclear reactors—Kashiwazaki-Kariwa 6 and 7—began operating in Japan in 1996.

- The majority of proposed nuclear reactors—those that have been ordered or are in the planning stages—are in Asian regions, including China, Japan, and the Republic of Korea. Of the last 39 reactors to come online, **28 were located in Asia**.

- China is slated to spend up to **$65 billion** to build nuclear facilities by 2020.

- In 2008 Japan launched its Fast Reactor Cycle Technology Development Project to bring **fast reactor technology** to commercial use.

- The nuclear industry faces a shortage of workers to design, build, and operate the next wave of nuclear plants. Due to intense recruitment efforts by the nuclear industry, enrollment in **four-year nuclear engineering programs** has increased in recent years.

- Recycling nuclear fuel could reuse a full **90 percent** of the energy that remains in the spent fuel rod, making the fuel cycle more efficient and reducing the volume of waste that requires permanent storage.

Nuclear Reactors Around the World, 2010

As of January 2010, more than 400 reactors were operating across the globe. With 104 operating units, the United States has the most reactors of any country in the world today. Construction of new reactors is underway in many other countries, particularly those in the Far East.

Country	Reactors Operable	Reactors under construction	Country	Reactors Operable	Reactors under construction
Argentina	2	1	Kazakhstan	0	0
Armenia	1	0	North Korea	0	0
Bangladesh	0	0	South Korea	20	6
Belarus	0	0	Lithuania	0	0
Belgium	7	0	Mexico	2	0
Brazil	2	0	Netherlands	1	0
Bulgaria	2	0	Pakistan	2	1
Canada	18	2	Poland	0	0
China	11	20	Romania	2	0
Czech Republic	6	0	Russia	31	9
Egypt	0	0	Slovakia	4	2
Finland	4	1	Slovenia	1	0
France	58	1	South Africa	2	0
Germany	17	0	Spain	8	0
Hungary	4	0	Sweden	10	0
India	18	5	Switzerland	5	0
Indonesia	0	0	Thailand	0	0
Iran	0	1	Turkey	0	0
Israel	0	0	Ukraine	15	0
Italy	0	0	UAE	0	0
Japan	54	1	United Kingdom	19	0
			USA	104	1

Source: World Nuclear Association, January 1, 2010. www.world-nuclear.org.

Nuclear Power in the Future

Many countries are turning to nuclear power to meet energy demands. When contrasted with planned or actual nuclear power plant construction in 2008, the International Atomic Energy Agency foresees the largest increases in deployment of nuclear power plants in Eastern Europe, the Middle East and South Asia, Africa, and the Far East.

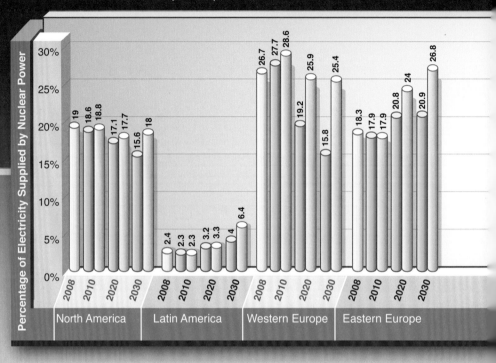

- In the United States most of the operating reactors—over 100—will likely be granted licenses to **extend their expected operating lives** from 30 or 40 years to 60 years.

- The nuclear industry is considering ways to increase the use of **thorium** as a nuclear fuel since it is more abundant in the earth's crust than is uranium, although thorium reactions are not as efficient as those produced by uranium.

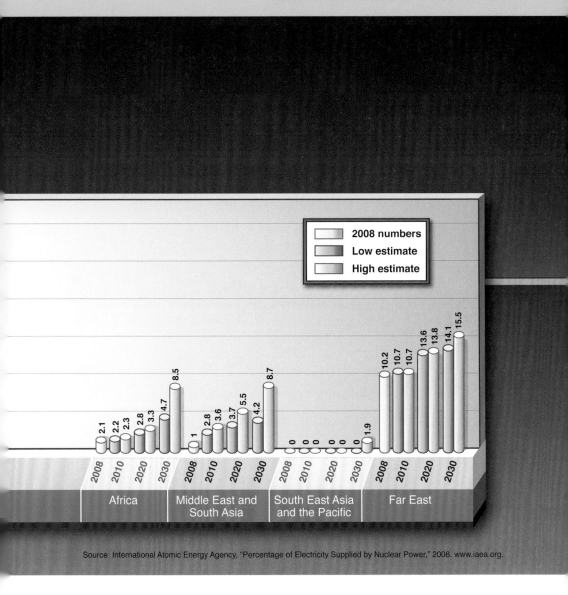

2008 numbers
Low estimate
High estimate

Africa: 2008 2.1, 2010 2.2, 2020 2.3, 2.8, 3.3, 2030 4.7, 8.5

Middle East and South Asia: 2008 1, 2010 2.8, 3.6, 2020 3.7, 5.5, 2030 4.2, 8.7

South East Asia and the Pacific: 2008 0, 2010 0, 2020 0, 2030 0, 0, 1.9

Far East: 2008 10.2, 2010 10.7, 10.7, 2020 13.6, 13.8, 2030 14.1, 15.5

Source: International Atomic Energy Agency, "Percentage of Electricity Supplied by Nuclear Power," 2008. www.iaea.org.

- Excluding Japan and France, there is about twice as much research and development expenditure worldwide on renewable energy sources, primarily **wind and solar**, compared to nuclear technology.

- The International Atomic Energy Agency estimates that the global nuclear power generating capacity will likely **double by the year 2030**.

Growing Support for Nuclear Power

According to a recent public opinion survey, support for nuclear power is growing in the United States.

Public Support for Nuclear Energy

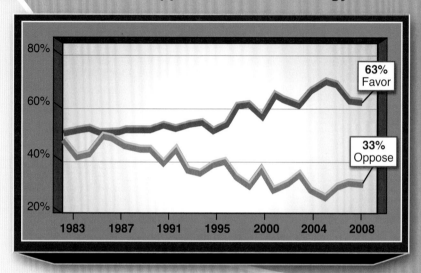

Public Support for Building More Nuclear Power Plants

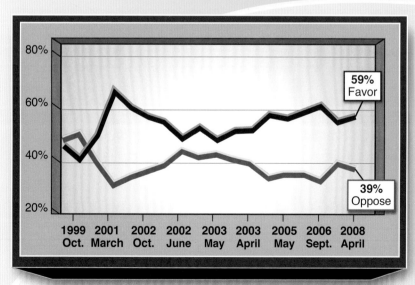

Source: Bisconti Research Inc./Nuclear Energy Institute, "Nuclear Energy: Just the Facts," May 2008. www.nei.org.

- In addition to the ITER International Fusion Energy Organization, a network of laboratories in Belgium, Brazil, Canada, China, the Czech Republic, Iran, Portugal, Russia, Thailand, and the United Kingdom is conducting joint projects to research **fusion and tokamak technology**.

- Cutting-edge design and **safety research** is currently underway at the Next Generation Nuclear Plant, an advanced test reactor at Idaho National Laboratory.

- According to the International Atomic Energy Agency, of the **30 countries** that use nuclear power to generate electricity, **24** have stated they will build new nuclear plants in coming years.

Key People and Advocacy Groups

American Nuclear Society (ANS): The ANS is a scientific and educational network of scientists, engineers, educators, and others who work to advance nuclear technology and its practical application.

Helen Caldicott: An outspoken critic of the nuclear industry, Caldicott, a physician, has written numerous articles and books and has founded many organizations in her mission to stop the spread of nuclear technology, in both the energy and military sector.

Pete Domenici: Former Republican senator from New Mexico Domenici served six terms before retiring in 2009. An avid supporter of nuclear power, Domenici was influential in passing the Energy Policy Act of 2005, which included $13 billion in subsidies for the nuclear power industry.

Dwight Eisenhower: The thirty-fourth U.S. president, Eisenhower delivered his famous Atoms for Peace speech to the United Nations in 1953. Subsequently, the United States launched a program to implement the peaceful use of atomic energy.

Enrico Fermi: An Italian physicist, Fermi is best known for his work that culminated in the first controlled, self-sustaining nuclear chain reaction at the University of Chicago in 1942.

International Atomic Energy Agency (IAEA): The IAEA was established as the Atoms for Peace organization in 1957. The agency works with member states worldwide to promote the peaceful and safe applications of nuclear technology.

Patrick Moore: A former activist with the environmental organization Greenpeace, Moore broke with the group in the 1980s and has since become an outspoken supporter of nuclear power. He helped found the Clean and Safe Energy Coalition, an organization that promotes the expansion of nuclear power.

Nuclear Energy Institute (NEI): The NEI is the policy organization of the nuclear energy industry, which promotes the beneficial uses of nuclear power through the national and global policy-making process.

Robert Oppenheimer: A physicist, Oppenheimer was the director of the Manhattan Project, the program that used nuclear technology to build the world's first atomic bomb at the Los Alamos National Laboratory during World War II.

Harry Reid: A Democratic senator from Nevada and the Senate majority leader since 2007, Reid worked for nearly two decades to block the construction of the congressionally designated Yucca Mountain nuclear waste repository. In 2009 construction came to a halt after President Barack Obama cut funding for the project.

Chronology

1932
English physicist James Chadwick discovers the neutron, an electrically uncharged particle.

1951
The Experimental Breeder Reactor-1 at the Idaho National Laboratory generates the world's first electricity produced from nuclear fission.

1954
The U.S. Congress amends the Atomic Energy Act to allow the Atomic Energy Commission to license private companies to build and operate nuclear power plants.

1942
Enrico Fermi and a team of scientists produce the first self-sustained nuclear chain reaction in a lab; the Manhattan Project, the U.S. Army's secret atomic energy program, is formed to build a nuclear bomb.

1955
A U.S. government reactor provides electricity to Arco, Idaho, making it the first town to be powered by nuclear energy.

1930   1940   1950   1960

1938
Physicists Otto Hahn and Fritz Strassmann of Germany split uranium atoms with a neutron to demonstrate nuclear fission.

1953
President Dwight Eisenhower proposes international cooperation for the peaceful applications of nuclear power in his Atoms for Peace speech before the General Assembly of the United Nations.

1957
The International Atomic Energy Agency is formed to promote peaceful uses of nuclear energy; the first U.S. commercial power plant begins operation in Shippingport, Pennsylvania, supplying power to Pittsburgh and areas of western Pennsylvania.

1945
In July the United States detonates the world's first atomic device near Alamogordo, New Mexico; in August the United States explodes atomic bombs on Hiroshima and Nagasaki in Japan, bringing World War II to a close.

1946
The U.S. Congress passes the Atomic Energy Act, creating the Atomic Energy Commission to oversee the postwar use and development of nuclear technology.

2010

The 436 nuclear power plants operating across the globe generate approximately 372 gigawatts of electricity. Over 50 reactors are under construction, including 20 in China, 9 in Russia, and 5 in India.

1979

A reactor at Three Mile Island nuclear plant near Harrisburg, Pennsylvania, suffers a partial core meltdown. No one is injured, and only a small quantity of radioactive material is released into the atmosphere.

1968

The Nuclear Nonproliferation Treaty is opened for signature. By 1986 more than 130 countries had signed the treaty, which seeks to halt the spread of nuclear materials and capabilities.

1992

The Energy Policy Act of 1992 makes key changes in the licensing process for nuclear power plants.

2002

Congress approves Yucca Mountain as the long-term repository for the nation's nuclear waste.

1960   1970   1980   1990   2000   2010

1974

The Energy Reorganization Act of 1974 replaces the Atomic Energy Commission with the Energy Research and Development Authority and the U.S. Nuclear Regulatory Commission. The latter is charged with overseeing the safe handling of nuclear materials.

2007

The U.S. Nuclear Regulatory Commission receives the first full nuclear power plant application in the United States in 28 years.

2009

President Barack Obama cuts funding for the Yucca Mountain repository; at the United Nations Summit on Climate Change, Obama calls for a cap on greenhouse gas emissions.

1986

An explosion occurs at the Chernobyl nuclear plant in Ukraine, representing the world's worst nuclear disaster to date. Massive amounts of radioactive materials are released and fallout occurs over large areas of Europe.

Related Organizations

American Nuclear Society (ANS)

555 N. Kensington Ave.

La Grange Park, IL 60526

phone: (800) 323-3044 • fax: (708) 352-0499

Web site: www.ans.org

The ANS is a nonprofit international, scientific, and educational organization established in 1954. The ANS promotes the safe application of nuclear science and technology and publishes numerous journals and magazines, including *Nuclear News* and the newsletter *ANS Standards News*.

Greenpeace

702 H St. NW

Washington, DC 20001

phone: (202) 462-1177

e-mail: info@wdc.greenpeace.org • Web site: www.greenpeace.org

Greenpeace is a nongovernmental network of environmental activists that opposes nuclear power on the grounds that it poses unacceptable risks to the environment, human health, and national security. Its Web site offers numerous reports, fact sheets, and articles.

International Atomic Energy Agency (IAEA)

PO Box 100

Wagramer Strasse 5

A-1400 Vienna, Austria

phone: (+431) 2600 0 • fax: (+431) 2600 7

e-mail: official.mail@iaea.org • Web site: www.iaea.org

The IAEA was created in 1957 to promote nuclear safety through inspections of existing nuclear facilities worldwide and through the dissemination of information and standards that promote safe and secure nuclear technologies. The IAEA publishes numerous periodicals, reports, and other documents.

Nuclear Energy Institute (NEI)

1776 I St. NW, Suite 400

Washington, DC 20006-3708

phone: (202) 739-8000 • fax: (202) 785-4019

Web site: www.nei.org

The NEI is the policy organization for the nuclear energy industry and participates in both the national and global policy-making process. NEI produces the monthly newsletter *Nuclear Energy Insight* as well as other reports.

Sierra Club

85 Second St.

San Francisco, CA 94105

phone: (415) 977-5500 • fax: (415) 977-5799

e-mail: information@sierraclub.org • Web site: www.sierraclub.org

Founded in 1892 by American conservationist John Muir, the Sierra Club is the oldest and largest grassroots environmental organization in the country. The group, which opposes nuclear power, works to reverse global warming and create a clean, renewable energy future. The Sierra Club publishes *Sierra* magazine and many books and articles.

Union of Concerned Scientists (UCS)

Two Brattle Sq.

Cambridge, MA 02238-9105

phone: (617) 547-5552 • fax: (617) 864-9405

Web site: www.ucsusa.org

The UCS is a nonprofit alliance that combines independent research and citizen advocacy in the pursuit of innovative and practical environmental solutions. The USC monitors the safety provisions of nuclear power plants in operation and assesses the risks of future plants. It publishes *Catalyst* magazine and numerous reports.

U.S. Department of Energy (DOE)

1000 Independence Ave. SW

Washington, DC 20585

phone: (202) 586-5000 • fax: (202) 586-4403

e-mail: the.secretary@hg.doe.gov • Web site: www.energy.gov

The DOE is a department of the federal government, created to advance national, economic, and energy security for the United States. It promotes scientific innovation and regulates policies related to energy and the handling of nuclear materials.

U.S. Environmental Protection Agency (EPA)

Ariel Rios Building

1200 Pennsylvania Ave. NW

Washington, DC 20460

phone: (202) 272-0167

Web site: www.epa.gov

The EPA was created by the federal government in 1970 to protect human health and the environment. The EPA develops and enforces regulations based on environmental laws passed by Congress and works with industry and state and local governments to control pollution, including radioactive wastes.

U.S. Nuclear Regulatory Commission (NRC)

Washington, DC 20555-0001

phone: (800) 368-5642

Web site: www.nrc.gov

The NRC was created by Congress in 1974 to regulate the civilian use of radioactive materials for peaceful purposes through licensing, inspection, and enforcement of its regulations. Its Web site offers many publications, including fact sheets and documents related to all phases of the nuclear fuel cycle.

World Nuclear Association (WNA)

22a St. James Sq.

London SW1Y 4JH

United Kingdom

phone: (+44) 20 74511520 • fax: (+44) 20 7839 1501

e-mail: wna@world-nuclear.org

The WNA is a worldwide network of companies representing the nuclear industry. The WNA provides a global forum for sharing information related to the nuclear fuel cycle and seeks to educate the public and promote wider acceptance of nuclear technology.

For Further Research

Books

David Bodansky, *Nuclear Energy: Principles, Practices, and Prospects*. New York: Springer, 2008.

Helen Caldicott, *Nuclear Power Is Not the Answer*. New York: New Press, 2006.

Gwyneth Cravens, *Power to Save the World: The Truth About Nuclear Energy*. New York: Knopf, 2007.

Alan M. Herbst and George W. Hopley, *Nuclear Energy Now: Why the Time Has Come for the World's Most Misunderstood Energy Source*. Hoboken, NJ: Wiley, 2007.

Ian Hore-Lacy, *Nuclear Energy in the 21st Century*. London: World Nuclear University Press, 2006.

James Mahaffey, *Atomic Awakenings: A New Look at the History and Future of Nuclear Power*. New York: Pegasus, 2009.

William Tucker, *Terrestrial Energy: How Nuclear Power Will Lead the Green Revolution and End America's Energy Odyssey*. Savage, MD: Bartleby, 2008.

J. Samuel Walker, *The Road to Yucca Mountain*. Berkeley and Los Angeles: University of California Press, 2009.

Periodicals

Ronald Bailey, "How Green Are Your Nukes?" *Reason*, February 2010.

Andrew Bast, "Energy Dependence," *Newsweek*, July 17, 2009.

David Biello, "Nuclear Power Reborn," *Scientific American*, September 26, 2007.

Ann S. Bisconti, "Climate Change and Our Energy Future," *Perspective on Public Opinion*, November 2009.

Gwyneth Cravens, "Is Nuclear Energy Our Best Hope?" *Discover*, May 2008.

Eduardo Cue, "How France Sees Its Nuclear Powered Future," *U.S. News & World Report*, March 10, 2009.

Kent Garber, "Lessons from the Yucca Mountain Nuclear Waste Storage Debate," *U.S. News & World Report*, March 16, 2009.

Michael Grunwald, "Nuclear's Comeback: Still No Energy Panacea," *Time*, December 31, 2008.

———, "Three Mile Island at 30: Nuclear Power's Pitfalls," *Time*, March 27, 2009.

Jason Mark, "Atomic Dreams," *Utne Reader*, January/February 2008.

Steven E. Miller and Scott D. Sagan, "Nuclear Power Without Nuclear Proliferation?" *Daedalus*, Fall 2009.

Burton Richter, "The Nuclear Option," *Newsweek*, July 7–14, 2008.

Theodore Rockwell, "Nuclear Energy: Not a Faustian Bargain, But a Near Perfect Providential Gift," *Nuclear News*, November 2008.

Elizabeth Svoboda, "New Technology Could Make Nuclear the Best Weapon Against Climate Change," *Discover*, June 2009.

Bryan Walsh, "Is Nuclear Power Viable?" *Time*, June 6, 2008.

Internet Sources

International Atomic Energy Agency, "Nuclear's Great Expectations," September 11, 2008. www.iaea.org/NewsCenter/News/2008/np 2008.html.

Brian Marshall and Robert Lamb, "How Nuclear Power Works," How Stuff Works, 2000. www.howstuffworks.com/nuclear-power.html.

Massachusetts Institute of Technology, "Update of the MIT 2003 Future of Nuclear Power: An Interdisciplinary MIT Study," 2009. http://web.mit.edu/nuclearpower/pdf/nuclearpower-update2009.pdf.

World Nuclear Association, "Waste Management," November 2007. www.world-nuclear.org/education/wast.html.

Source Notes

Overview

1. Quoted in Caterino Dutto, "Einstein's Nuclear Warning," The Carnegie Endowment for International Peace, 2010. www.carnegieendowment.org.
2. Quoted in Pete V. Domenici, *A Brighter Tomorrow: Fulfilling the Promise of Nuclear Energy*. New York: Rowman & Littlefield, 2004, p. 1.
3. Domenici, *A Brighter Tomorrow*, p. 27.
4. Quoted in Richard Curtis and Elizabeth Hogan, *Nuclear Lessons: An Examination of Nuclear Power's Safety, Economic, and Political Record*. Harrisburg, PA: Stackpole, 1980, p. 164.
5. James Lovelock, "Our Nuclear Lifeline," *Reader's Digest*, March 2005.
6. Jim Riccio, "Risky Business: The Probability and Consequences of a Nuclear Accident," Greenpeace, March 14, 2008. www.greenpeace.org.

Is Nuclear Power a Viable Energy Source?

7. Quoted in Richard Rhodes, *Nuclear Renewal*. New York: Viking, 1993, p. 33.
8. Quoted in Rhodes, *Nuclear Renewal*, p. 37.
9. Domenici, *A Brighter Tomorrow*, p. 2.
10. Quoted in Nuclear Energy Institute, "Need for New Nuclear Plants," December 2009. www.nei.org.
11. Peter W. Huber and Mark P. Mills, *The Bottomless Well: The Twilight of Fuel, the Virtue of Waste, and Why We Will Never Run Out of Energy*. New York: Basic, 2005, p. 170.
12. Arjun Makhijani, executive summary to *Carbon Free and Nuclear Free: A Roadmap for U.S. Energy Policy*, Institute for Energy and Environmental Research, July 2007. www.ieer.org.
13. Al Gore, *Our Choice: A Plan to Solve the Climate Crisis*. Emmaus, PA: Rodale, 2009, p. 155.
14. Congressional Budget Office, "Nuclear Power's Role in Generating Electricity," May 2008. www.cbo.gov.

How Does Nuclear Power Affect the Environment?

15. Intergovernmental Panel on Climate Change, "Climate Change 2007: Synthesis Report," November 2007. www.ipcc.ch.
16. Richard L. Garwin and Georges Charpak, *Megawatts and Megatons: A Turning Point in the Nuclear Age?* New York: Knopf, 2001, p. 5.
17. International Atomic Energy Agency, "Climate Change and Nuclear Power 2008," December 2008. www.iaea.org.
18. Nuclear Energy Institute, "Nuclear Energy's Vital Role in Reducing Greenhouse Gas Emissions," July 25, 2008. www.nei.org.
19. Patrick Moore, "Going Nuclear: A Green Makes the Case," *Washington Post*, April 16, 2006. www.washingtonpost.com.
20. Nuclear Information and Resource Service, "False Promises: Debunking Nuclear Industry Propaganda," May 2008. www.nirs.org.
21. Michio Kaku and Jennifer Trainer, eds., *Nuclear Power: Both Sides; The Best Arguments For and Against the Most Controversial Technology*. New York: Norton, 1982, p. 113.
22. Gwyneth Cravens, *Power to Save the World: The Truth About Nuclear En-*

ergy. New York: Knopf, 2007, p. 269.

Is Nuclear Power Safe?

23. Riccio, "Risky Business."
24. Quoted in U.S. Nuclear Regulatory Commission, "The Third Annual Homeland Security Summit Session on 'The Best-Laid Plans: A Case Study in Preparedness Planning,'" June 3, 2004. www.nrc.org.
25. Physicians for Social Responsibility, "Dirty, Dangerous, and Expensive: The Truth About Nuclear Power," 2009. www.psr.org.
26. Huber and Mills, *The Bottomless Well*, p. 169.

27. Gore, *Our Choice*, p. 161.

What Is the Future of Nuclear Power?

28. Domenici, *A Brighter Tomorrow*, p. 215.
29. Quoted in UCSD Jacobs School of Engineering, "Plasma Power: Turning Fusion into a Renewable Energy Source," September 11, 2009. www.jacobsschool.ucsd.edu.
30. ITER, "ITER and the Environment," 2009. www.iter.org.
31. Huber and Mills, *The Bottomless Well*, pp. 169–70.

List of Illustrations

Index

accidents
    industrial, rate at U.S. nuclear plants, 62
    nuclear, improvement in reactor safety after,
        18–19, 53
Advisory Committee on Uranium, 11
Areva reprocessing plant (La Hague, France), 42
    annual amount of spent fuel processed by, 47
atomic age, birth of, 10–12
Atomic Energy Act (1946), 12, 13
Atomic Energy Commission, 12, 13, 18, 21
Atoms for Peace program, 12–13

Barnaby, Frank, 72
Beasley, J. Barney, Jr., 21
The Boone and Crockett Club, 44
The Bottomless Well: The Twilight of Fuel, the
    Virtue of Waste, and Why We Will Never Run
    Out of Energy (Huber and Mills), 25–26, 70
breeder reactors, 15, 66–67
A Brighter Tomorrow: Fulfilling the Promise of
    Nuclear Energy (Domenici), 16, 22

Caldicott, Helen, 21
carbon dioxide (CO_2), 18, 19, 36–37
    emissions avoided in U.S. by alternative
        energy sources, 47 (chart)
    incentives to reduce emissions of may favor
        nuclear power, 25, 27
    reduced emissions from improved efficiency of
        U.S. nuclear power plants, 46
Carter, Jimmy, 42
Census Bureau, U.S., 22
Charpak, Georges, 37
Chernobyl accident (Ukraine, 1986), 18, 22, 60
    number of cancer deaths related to, 51, 54
China, spending on nuclear facilities by, 74
The China Syndrome (film), 60
coal, 28, 38
    energy efficiency of, uranium *vs.,* 13
    percent of worldwide electricity generated
        by, 23
    waste from combustion of, nuclear power
        waste *vs.,* 40
Concerned Citizens for Nuclear Safety, 58
Corradini, Michael, 64
Cowley, Stephen, 73
Cravens, Gwyneth, 40

deaths
    cancer

        from bombing of Hiroshima/Nagasaki, 20
        related to Chernobyl accident, 51, 54
    from fossil-fuel pollution, 19
Department of Energy, U.S. (DOE), 42, 65
deuterium, 68
Diaz, Nils, 51–52
Doerner, Russ, 68–69
Domenici, Pete, 16, 22, 65

Einstein, Albert, 11
Eisenhower, Dwight, 12–13
electricity
    global generation of, by source, 34 (chart)
    nuclear-generated
        amount worldwide, 20
        current and projected, by world region,
            76–77 (chart)
        as percent of total, by nation, 33 (chart)
        as percent of total energy, 15
        sources of, in 2007, 23
        U.S. productions costs, by source, 35
            (chart)
Electric Power Research Institute, 23, 53
energy
    efficiency of coal *vs.* uranium, 13
    growth in demand for, 22–23
    percent of total North American production
        from renewable *vs.* nuclear sources, 25
    requirements for nuclear fusion, 69
Energy Multiplier Module (EM2), 67–68
Environmental Protection Agency (EPA), 30,
    37, 50
European Repository Development
    Organisation, 46

fast breeder reactors, 66–67
Fast Reactor Cycle Technology Development
    Project (Japan), 74
Fermi, Enrico, 11–12, 14
fission, 8
    discovery of, 10–12
fossil fuels, 15
    deaths from pollution by, 19
    depletion of, 16
France, nuclear power in, 24, 59
fusion, 68–69

Garwin, Richard L., 37
Generation IV International Forum, 65
global warming, 17–18

Index

About the Author

Jill Karson is a writer and editor. She lives in Carlsbad, California, with her husband and three children.